THE GENDER WARS TRILOGY

THE GENDER WARS TRILOGY

*Medea * Jason *
A Marriage Made in Hell*

Ian Kluge

Copyright © 2005 by Ian Kluge.

Library of Congress Number:		2003098751
ISBN :	Softcover	1-4134-3556-4

All rights reserved. No part of this book may be reproduced or transmitted in any form or by any means, electronic or mechanical, including photocopying, recording, or by any information storage and retrieval system, without permission in writing from the copyright owner.

This book was printed in the United States of America.

To order additional copies of this book, contact:
Xlibris Corporation
1-888-795-4274
www.Xlibris.com
Orders@Xlibris.com
20747

CONTENTS

PREFACE 7

MEDEA..13

JASON 62

A MARRIAGE MADE IN HELL... 120

PREFACE

Like Arthur Miller's *The Crucible*, *The Gender Wars Trilogy* gives extreme views and emotions an opportunity to deconstruct themselves and reveal their underlying nature and dynamics. The trilogy is grounded in the debates that exploded in the early 1970's when a number of women authors forcefully challenged all aspects of past and present thinking about gender. Friedan, Millett, Brownmiller, Daly, Dworkin, MacKinnon, Steinem, Kristeva, and Faludi to name only a few of the most prominent, seized control of the feminist movement, the topics and even language of debate as well as the tactics of re-dressing perceived historical wrongs. These radicals so successfully captured the public's and law-makers' attention that rational critiques and cautions voiced by moderate women made little headway and, like Christina Hoff Sommers' *Who Stole Feminism?*, were often vilified as betrayals of womankind. Men's responses were effectively absent, the work of Warren Farrell and Robert Bly notwithstanding.

Two plays of the trilogy—*Medea* and *Jason*—reflect the emotional, intellectual and social turmoil that revolutionized gender relations since the 1970's and still shapes modern western culture. The third play—*A Marriage Made in Hell*—deals with the need for reconciliation. In the original myth, of course, no such reconciliation takes place; however, it is impossible to reflect on the story without asking whether any rapprochement *could* ever have happened between the two protagonists, and if so, on what basis. *A Marriage Made in Hell* answers those questions.

Although *The Gender Wars Trilogy* deals specifically with the gender wars engulfing western societies since the 1970's, it does have a wider message, namely, that ideologies and the ideological mind-set diminish the humanity of their proponents and turn them into living parodies of a truly human(e) being. The matter is best explained as follows. All people have ideas and beliefs about the nature of reality, that is, they have a mental 'map' of the world. As their life experience unfolds, most people make changes to this map so that their map conforms at least somewhat to reality, the 'territory'. However, there are some people, 'ideologues', who are so overwhelmingly committed to a political, social or economic ideology that they struggle to make the territory conform to their mental map. They have given up on the dialogue or dialectic between the map and the territory and have made an unreserved one-sided commitment to the map under any and all circumstances. The problem, of course, is that life is messier, more complex, than any ideas we can have about it and that when our efforts to make life conform to our map become too strenuous, too fanatical, we end up with 'monstrosities', inhumane extremes of thought, feeling and action. Both Medea and Jason are ideologues of the gender wars.

The first play, *Medea*, presents the title character re-telling the story of her relationship with Jason from a radical feminist point of view. As the archetypal 'wronged woman' in Greek mythology, but also as a proud and effective fighter, Medea is the ideal character to speak for the radical 'new woman' of our time. However, she is not merely a collage of major feminists and a mouth-piece for their ideas: she is a passionate, powerful, highly intelligent, highly articulate woman with a lively sense of humor and a gift for dramatics to communicate her vision. Indeed, for those who appreciate the company of strong characters, she is a likeable person who refuses to soft-pedal her views and emotions. She is absolutely sincere in her beliefs, but her sincerity is unmodified by any rational self-critique which is why she tends to indulge in emotional outbursts and outrageous flights of intellectual fantasy. Moreover, she is tortured by her own ambivalent feelings about men; in theory, she feels obligated to hate them, but in actual fact, she is deeply in love with Jason right to the end. She is particularly galled by Glauce's success with "men magic", and murders her at least partly out of jealousy for stealing Jason.

Unlike traditional versions of the story, *Medea* draws attention to the vicious and even murderous streak in Medea's nature. Even though Euripedes and Ovid (among others) over-look her determined ruthlessness, the fact remains that she personally murders her younger brother Absyrtus, her two sons and Glauce and is directly responsible for the deaths of Pelias and his daughters. She may have suffered at Jason's hands, but she is no squeamish, helpless woman, no mere victim. This makes her especially apt to represent contemporary feminism which, despite its obvious successes as a militant ideology, has never faced up to the ruthless streak in its character. Admittedly, some feminist splinter groups have tried to distance themselves from this aspect of feminism but they have never seriously influenced the movement as a whole which not only wages war on masculine privilege but also mercilessly castigates and marginalizes those women who prefer traditional roles.

Medea was first presented in Prince George, British Columbia, in October, 1998 and has appeared at different times in Vancouver, Victoria and Prince George, British Columbia. Kendra Patton played Medea in each case. The play was produced by Ursa Major Theatre ("Theatre With Teeth").

Jason gives voice to the powerful and confidently entrenched male, who, if there were a viable counter-part to the feminist movement, might be called a radical masculinist. Though less emotional than Medea, he is no less extreme in his views. Like her, he is witty and intellectually incisive as well as nasty, rude and provocative; like her, he has valid insights into the human condition, and, although he sees himself as a 'man of reason', like her he suffers from an inability to assess his ideas self-critically. He sees no real need for significant change in gender relations. Fully at home in his maleness, he believes that the male-dominated societies that seem to be the global norm are the natural results of human evolution and, for all their apparent injustices, ultimately serve the greater long-term good of all men and women. With considerable pride, he asserts that he, like all males, is a hunter and killer and that the only difference among men is in what they hunt: meat, adventure, ideas or in rare cases, God. Furthermore, he is convinced that in their heart of hearts most, if not all, women want men like him—because such men ensure the survival of them and their children. As defender of the 'natural order', Jason sees and presents himself as the voice of all men—and all women who reject the ideology of radical feminism in theory and/or practice.

Whereas Medea's strategy is to make revolutionary change by force of sheer moral outrage, Jason's strategy is to let nature take its course since he believes that in its essential features at least, the old order of gender relations reflects the requirements of survival in our evolutionary natural environment. Jason sees himself as a Taoist or, as he puts it, a sailor, who succeeds because he works in harmony with nature, not against it. In his view, Medea is a sorceress, someone who tries to enforce her merely human will against the natural order of things. This perceived alliance with nature is the source of the arrogant self-confidence and humor with which Jason responds to Medea's arguments, plans and visions. He thinks her ideas and schemes are mere brain fantasies, airy nothings doomed to be burst by the harsh realities of the natural order.

Jason originally appeared in Prince George, British Columbia in August, 2000 with Corey Hicks in the title role. Later productions featured John Stuart. The play was produced by Ursa Major Theatre ("Theatre With Teeth").

In the traditional Greek myth, Medea and Jason part ways and never meet again. The original story notwithstanding, *A Marriage Made in Hell*, re-unites them despite their vigorous resistance. The play, in which the author presides at a marriage ceremony to which the audience is 'invited', shows Medea and Jason reluctantly learning that their re-union is a matter of deep necessity, that no matter how much they might like to, they cannot escape each other, and that they must make changes to their 'maps' of reality if they wish to retain their humanity. However, this ending is bitter-sweet, not romantic. All is not suddenly 'made good' or forgiven. Rather, Medea and Jason embark on their new lives only under the greatest pressure. At the end, they leave together as Milton's Adam and Eve left paradise: knowing that there was little real choice for them but to begin again and that the way ahead would be difficult. Other characters such as their sons, Glauce, Aetes, and Hecabe open Medea and Jason to a more humane, less ideologically driven, view of existence.

Watching *The Gender Wars Trilogy* requires the audience to remain detached, to avoid personally identifying with either of the two protagonists. A viewer who succumbs to identification with them will miss not only their galling partisan self-righteousness but also the network of self-contradictions, self-serving hypocrisies, over-generalizations and mere assumptions that undermines their self-presentations. With them, what you see is definitely not what you get. Both *Medea* and *Jason* are razor-edged satires of the attitudes and beliefs they ostensibly advocate. Only Glauce—even as presented by Medea and Jason—is a figure of sympathy insofar as she is more sanely balanced that either of the protagonists. The third play, *A Marriage Made in Hell*, presents various characters with whom a viewer can sympathize if for no other reason than that they do not view life with ideological blinders. They struggle heroically to make Jason and Medea see the human complexities overlooked or ruthlessly discarded by their ideologies.

Ian Kluge

MEDEA

A MODERN OFFICE WITH A FEW PLANTS AND FLOWERS ON REPLICAS OF GREEK COLUMNS. MEDEA IS ALREADY ON STAGE WHEN THE AUDIENCE ENTERS, SITTING IN A SWIVEL CHAIR WITH HER BACK TO THE AUDIENCE. WHEN THE PLAY STARTS, SHE TURNS TO FACE THE AUDIENCE.

They call me a bitch—the biggest bitch ever.
Well, I sure as hell hope so.
Megabitch—
With teeth this long.
There's no other way
For women to get respect.
Meet the dinks on their own turf.
Bite—and bite hard
'Cause men don't have ears—
They have to be added by surgery
—Bitch surgery—
And I'm the bitch surgeon-in-chief!

SHE GETS UP AND ADVANCES TOWARDS THE AUDIENCE.

It's a damn good thing you women
Have learned that lesson at last.
I'm proud of you—really I am.
You're finishing up what I started
Three thousand years ago . . .

I guess in a way, I'm your mother.
And you're all the daughters I never had in my life.
I was cursed with sons
—Two of them—
But I slit their throats.
I *saved* them from being rapists.
Like all other men.

So *you're* my daughters,
'Cause you understand it's war—
Holy war!
Them
Against *us!*

No quarter asked—and none given,
And the losers end up as slaves.
But, let me warn you—
Don't ever get suckered into equality.
There's no such thing as equality in this world,
And if there is
It's not worth a fuck—
Unless you want to live your whole life
In a Mexican stand-off . . .

In this world, you're either one up
Or one down.
You've got the whip in your hand
Or you don't.
You choose.
I did—
And look at me.
I'm a free woman.
Empowered.
Respected.
Feared.

Hated.
I tell you, if you're not hated
You're nothing.
And not just by men.
By women too.

Let's face it, most women are cows,
Glad to groan under some bull
And shit out his calves.
And these cows, let me tell you,
And these poor, stupid cows,
Who really believe they're happy,
Unless they fear you
Will gore you to death.
They'll rip you open from asshole to breakfast,
All in the name of 'family love' and their bulls.

Free women like me
—And you—
Are a threat to their happy slavery.
They can't imagine life
Without penises, sperm and brats,
And tits dripping with milk.
Cows dressed up as women,
That's what they are . . .

As if being a woman
Had something to do with brats
And 'love', and all that nurturing shit!
I hate them as much as I hate
Jason and everything male.

Which leads me to this *fantastic* discovery:
Hate and disgust
Are *fabulous* aphrodisiacs!
Turns ons.

I mean it!
If you hate hard, *really* hard,
If you're disgusted enough,
You'll get an orgasm of *pure hatred,*
That makes your hot little cunt
Explode
Like fireworks
Into new worlds of pleasure—
Without men
Or dildo's,
A perfectly feminine orgasm
Created *by* our own bodies
In our own bodies,
For our own bodies.
Orgasm
Without slavery to men
Or anything else like—'love'.

I was 'in love' once.
Really.
So it's not like I don't have experience.
You know what 'love' is for women?
Slavery!
To cunts crying for bulls,
Wombs crying for calves,
Breasts aching for little mouths,
Eyes hungry for goo-goo smiles
And togetherness.
Never alone,
Not even when you're alone.
It's like you're possessed by demons.
Whoever invented love *hated* women!
I learned that the hard way.
All women do—
Especially the first time.

I was eighteen when it happened
And thought it was wonderful.

LAUGHS.

You know, at that time
I was making love potions for others!
I wanted everyone
To have all the happiness I imagined—
But what did I really *know* about love?

Naturally, being young, I thought I knew everything!
I mean, I was a moon-priestess—
Wasn't I famous already for magic?
Couldn't I draw down the moon
And make it float like a beautiful pearl on the sea?
Couldn't I make stones speak
And rivers run backwards?
I thought knowledge
Would save me from being a fool.
Ha!
Knowledge can't save a woman from slavery to love.
Only *hate* can do that.

Love is the traitor waiting inside every woman!
Waiting.
Plotting.
Scheming.
The truth is, a woman's heart
Is a trap
To deliver her into slavery.

Which proves that god is a man!
No woman would do this to herself.
Or others.

But, being eighteen,
I was happy and wise in my ignorance,
Proud, untouched by that sickness
—Until *he* arrived—
Jason . . .
Because of that stupid fleece.

You see, my father, the King of Colchis,
Had a golden fleece which he got from his father
Who got it from—
Never mind, I'll spare you the story.
But as long as he had the fleece
The kingdom was safe.
But
—As always with gods and men—
There was a catch.
The gods decreed that anyone, rich or poor,
Woman or man, had the right
To steal that fleece.

Well, you can imagine
It was well guarded.
There was a dragon that never slept
Curled round the tree where it hung.
That dragon had teeth *this* long,
And breath that stank like a mid-summer shit-house.
But even before you got to the dragon,
You had to get past these man-eating oxen
With their blast-furnace breath
And hooves of razor-sharp brass.
If you got past them
—And nobody ever did—
You had to sow a field with these magical teeth
That turned into thousands of soldiers
All wanting to kill you.

Anyone with a speck of plain common-sense
Wouldn't go *near* that place.
But, you know how it is with people:
As soon as they can't have something
They want it!
They came from all over the world
Like flies to poisoned honey,
Willing, *eager* to die . . .

One of them told my father
The dragon was just an illusion,
A kind of hallucination,
And so were the man-eating oxen.
Why, he'd just snap his hypnotic fingers
And pfitt!—they'd be gone.
Well, pfitt!
He was gone.
I remember those meat-eating oxen
Belching and farting for days
And father and all his lords laughing . . .
I have to admit
I laughed as hard as the rest . . .

*ADOPTS A SOFTER TONE SHOWING THAT SHE WAS AT
LEAST A LITTLE IN LOVE WITH HIM.*

And of course, the poet.
Not much older than me,
With a voice of God-given beauty,
And verses that left you breathless.
Why *he* wanted the fleece, *I'll* never know.
He didn't need gold to be famous or rich.
He just needed his voice,
And he had that already.
I've often wondered what sickness
Brought him to our door.

According to him
His verses would charm those oxen
And heal the rage of the dragon.
He said it was only hurt,
Had suffered some terrible wound as a dragon-child
And couldn't sleep for the pain.
And those earth-born soldiers—
Why, they just wanted
Someone to sing to them softly.

When he spoke with that wonderful voice
We almost believed him.
Father's face darkened with worry—
Imagine!
The Golden Fleece
Won by a poet!
The dragon, a small hurt child
Grown monstrous with pain,
The oxen, mere cows after all,
And the soldiers, just bad little boys
Who wanted a lullaby.

Father spit in his face
Hoping he'd do something stupid
So they could kill him.
But the poet just wiped off the spit
And whispered, "Like others,
I too have a right."
Father exploded, "Tomorrow then, poet!
Come for your right tomorrow!"

He did.

I could have helped him.
I knew how to get past the oxen,
The dragon . . . the soldiers . . .
He deserved to live.

The world would have been
A more beautiful place with his verses,
But I was eighteen—
I wanted
—I *needed*—
More.
Action,
Excitement,
Something
—Someone—
A little dangerous
To stir up my blood, to—
I didn't know what.

Well, not until Jason arrived . . .

SHE SPEAKS AS IF SWEPT AWAY BY THE MEMORIES.

Hair, golden as sunlight,
Muscles, rippling like waves,
And those good-little-bad-boy looks.
My knees turned to water.
I hardly dared breathe when he spoke.

You know, he was almost laughing.
"Aetes!" he called, "Great King!
My name is Jason.
I've come for the Golden Fleece!"
As if it were only a parcel!

I stared so hard I nearly fell over!
He saw me—and smiled.
My blood turned to steam,
I nearly fainted, not just from desire,
But wanting to *be* with that man!
Only with him could I really *be*,
Only with *him* was I *real!*

I would have embraced him right there,
But my nurse—the old crow—
Held onto my wrist with her claws,
And smiled.
She smiled,
For Medea the proud young witch
Was discovering what it meant
To be Medea, the woman . . .

That night she brought me a message,
From *him:*
"Your lion is here to be tamed."
I didn't know what it meant.
I didn't care.
It was from him—to *me!*
He knew I existed!
Nothing else mattered
And so that same night
Disguised as a servant I sneaked to his camp.
Of course, his guards caught me.
They threw me into his tent like a bundle of rags.
Why not?
I was only a woman,
Like all the others who came to his tent.
Stupid heifers, sick for heroic semen . . .

Yes, I was one of them—once.
Just a walking hole,
Tortured by all that emptiness in my belly—
Fill it up, Jason.
Drive your bung into my barrel!
And don't you forget
To leave me a little memento!
There's unused room in my guts.
And I've got these tits
Dying for paws and a mouth . . .
O gawd, gawd, gawd!

They say I'm unnatural . . .
I hear them when I walk by,
"Bzz bzzz,
Bzz. Bzzz,
Unnatural woman!"

Of course I'm unnatural—
Why the hell shouldn't I be?
Have you ever seen what nature does to us women?
Bleeding each month,
A 'wise wound' they call it—
O sure, if wisdom is being cramped over,
And bloated, like a soaked sponge.
You hate the whole fucking world.
And then, when it stops,
You puke the good news all around!
You've got this worm-thing inside you.
A parasite, stealing your strength,
And not just your strength—
Your freedom,
Your power,
Your *pride*.

And then, of course, child-birth.
O yes!
Shit.
Pain.
Piss.
And blood—
For what?
A baby!
For more shit and piss
And then you start leaking milk,
And before you know it, you're bleeding again—

Just leaky barrels with all kinds of holes—
That's what we women are!
Nature *hates* women!
And every free woman,
Every woman with pride
Hates nature!

If women want to be free,
We must *defy* nature!
If we want real power,
We must strangle our 'natural' instincts!
If we want our own lives,
We must *murder* our children
Even before they are born!
That's how it is
Unless we want to be slaves
To nature and men
Or their stand-ins,
Like government hand-outs.
Social assistance they call it—
Ha!
It means you've married the government.
You're a slave
To a pen-pushing bastard behind a desk!
He doesn't care who you fuck with—
As long as you dance to *his* tune
The rest of the time.

The hard, brutal, *natural* fact is,
The most helpless thing in the world
Is a woman with brats.
And that's what it all comes down to—
Dependence!
Real freedom for women,
Real freedom means telling nature
And all the gods to fuck off!

Anything less is just selling yourself . . .

Like I did.
Crawling to Jason's tent, crying,
"Please! Let me help you!"
I showed him my gifts,
A magical ointment to shield his skin
From those man-eating oxen,
Moon-oil to put the sleepless dragon to sleep,
And a crystal to throw at the soldiers.
"They'll blame each other
And slaughter themselves."

We married that night,
And he promised to love me forever.

What man with a stiff cock doesn't?

And I,
Like every woman enslaved by love
Promised to be his bride . . .

*TRIUMPHANTLY. SHE LIKES WINNING NO MATTER
WHAT THE 'GAME' IS.*

Next day
Jason hi-jacked the fleece
—With my help—
And we sailed away on the Argo.

But father's boats were behind us,
His whole damn navy
And if they caught us, I knew how we'd die.
Father had this huge frying pan in the palace,
He'd oil us and fry us alive,
Slowly, to bring out the flavor . . .

That's when I put my secret plan into action.
You see, I brought my young brother Absyrtus along.
I told him it was a boat race and I was rooting for Jason.
One look at the Argo
—She was a beautiful ship—
And he would have killed to come.
I mean, he was only ten.

When my father's ships got too close

SHE MAKES A SLITTING MOTION AS SHE SPEAKS.

I grabbed him and slit his throat.

SHE PAUSES BRIEFLY.

He screamed once, maybe twice.
Remember, I'm a moon-priestess—
I've done it to hundreds of rams
So it went pretty quick.
Then I chopped him to pieces,
And threw the bits into the sea.
Sort of like . . . stewing beef.

That, I am proud to say,
Is the closest I've come to cooking!

Just as I planned, my father went for the bait.
He slowed down his ships to pick up the pieces.
Our people believe
If you're not buried on land,
You become a ghost
And wander in pain forever.
And so, while daddy was fishing
The Argo escaped.

And that's when I started to see what was going on.

Slowly, of course.
It took me a while before I had enough guts
To really see what I saw.
But it started then, my path to freedom,
With fear in the Argonauts' eyes.

After Absyrtus, they were afraid,
Not because I was Jason's wife
But because I was *me*—
A woman who'd killed a male.

I heard them grumbling,
"She'll slit our throats while we sleep,
She'll feed our pricks to the fish."

A woman who wasn't afraid to kill men
Made *them* afraid,
And you've got to remember,
These were professional killers.
Two of them went to Jason.
They told him I was unnatural,
Maybe a demon,
And offered to kill me.
"You've had your fun with her, boss.
And you've got the fleece!
So, give her to us for a while
And then—splash!"

They laughed.

I thought he'd kill them right there.
I thought he'd castrate the buggers
And make them chew on their nuts,
Saw them in half from crotch to the eyeballs—
But he only laughed.

He *laughed,*
And when he finished, you know what he said?
"She's a perfectly natural woman.
Look. All of her crimes are *love-crimes.*
She's betrayed her father, her mother, her country—
For what?
Love!
She's murdered her own little brother—
For love,
And her unborn children.
That sounds like a natural woman to me!
If you're lucky, you'll get one just like her!"
And then they all laughed again,
At me—at *all* women . . .

*SHE MOVES CLOSE TO THE AUDIENCE AS IF ADDRESSING
EVERYONE PERSONALLY.*

Have you ever had a moment of vision,
A sudden instant when everything's clear as a crystal?
Right then I saw the whole fucking disaster.
I saw how women were slaves
To their bodies, their feelings,
And how the desire for love and children
Made us betray ourselves
Into the hands of men.
And I saw how men
Made full use of our weakness.
And all of a sudden, I understood
This was a war.
Men
Against women.
And women, instead of drawing their daggers
Just opened their legs!
For an instant I saw,

Not just the vicious depravity of men and everything male
—Forever poking and prodding at every hole—
But the pathetic wretchedness of all women.
It was *so easy* to fool us,
So easy to keep us enslaved—
Because we adored our chains!

Who is less free than a captive who *wants* to be captured?
What fools women were,
Blinding ourselves to the truth,
Happy prisoners dancing in chains!
Helpless, powerless, lacking all pride,
So degraded we don't even know
We've lost the whole fucking war!

Remember what happened at Lemnos,
That island in the Aegean?

When we arrived, the women had not seen men
For over five years.
They'd murdered them all
And founded a women's republic,
Run by, and for, women.

Of course, the men were to blame.
They said their wives stank, meaning
—What else?—
Their wives were no longer happy sexual serfs.
They wanted to do something better than shitting out brats!

So, what did their husbands do?
They got new cows,
A bunch of dumb broads who believed all the lies,
Woman as 'nurturer', woman as 'spiritual healer',

The patter of little feet.
Goo-goo eyes, shit and new little hopes for the world
O gawd, gawd, gawd!
Just saying it makes me puke . . .

Anyway, so their wives pretended remorse,
We're sorry, boo-boo, sniff-sniff, and got them to bed—
And killed them!
Real kitchen work for once.
Stab, slice, slit, dice, hack—
That night
It was men bleeding into the sheets!

The collaborationist cows
Were told to abort
Or ship out on a raft.
Most took the raft—
Dumb cunts!

When the Argo arrived at Lemnos, it wasn't pretty.
Five years without men and nature had taken revenge.
Those women were crazy with lust.
They were so desperate, so giddy for anything male,
Jason just said,
"Go make 'em women again."

They didn't need telling twice.

It was the most shameful week of my life.
Those man-crazy cats were like a mirror to me,
Reflecting my own enslavement to nature,
My own dependence on men.

They were fucking in every corner.
Screaming and fighting
For every man, every squirt of sperm.

They had no pride, no dignity,
Nothing but sheer, raw, primitive instinct and lust.
I saw friendships destroyed, freedom trampled—
As plain as my own two hands, I saw
The degradation of women
When they surrender to nature,
And give in to 'love' and all that motherhood shit.

And I saw how the men took advantage.
They got good times and sore cocks,
And the women got fifteen years
Of slavery to men and their brats.

On Lemnos, I *knew*—
History was a plot,
A conspiracy among men
To enslave all women,
To keep us stupid and weak,
Without pride or power,
A plot to suppress our *real* wishes,
Our *real* ambitions and talents,
To keep us happy just being the family cow . . .

I said this to Jason,
And he—just laughed, goddamn it!
He was always laughing at me.

He gives me this lecture like I'm a dumb little girl.
He was always giving me lectures.

*SHE GIVES A MOCKING RE-ENACTMENT OF JASON'S
SPEECHES.*

"You talk like a spoiled little princess
Who's never been far from the palace.
Go into the world and you'll see
History is a plot, all right.

And everyone's plotting the same bloody thing—
To survive until morning,
To escape disease and starvation.
It's a plot
To live through the next earthquake or drought
And, above all, to make sure your children
—At least one or two—
Live long enough
To look after you when you're old—
If, that is, you get old . . ."

Then he blabbers on, "Remember,
Women are lucky.
They get to be slaves and make babies.
Men get to fight for the women—and die.
Rape is survivable, dear.
Disembowelment is not."

He talked like a pompous ass
—Men always do—
When passing on 'wisdom' to women.
"*I've* been in the world, *I've* seen how *real* people live.
They don't have time or strength
To play all the games you imagine.
They're practical, down-to-earth people,
They do what it takes to keep living.
To them every child is a gift
That raises the odds of survival.
And those women,
Real women
—Not spoiled little palace flowers—
Would be insulted by your suggestion
They're too stupid and weak
To figure out how to kill men
In their sleep, or cut off their pricks.

THE GENDER WARS TRILOGY

If those women put up with what you call 'shit'
They've got good reasons.
Otherwise, what are you saying—
That *you're* the first intelligent woman?
The *first* one ever to notice what's going on?
Were all your foremothers only whipped bitches and fools?"

And he laughed.

God, how I hated him then!
He laughed in my face and said,
"That's hubris, Medea, damnable pride
Be careful—it's the one crime
The gods never forgive . . ."

You know what I said?
"Fuck God!
Fuck the gods!"
And for once, for the first bloody time,
He didn't laugh . . .

He tries to scare me instead,
The way you scare little kids with boogey-man stories.
"Medea, be careful
You—and I—are just human,
But the gods are superior forces.
Like the ocean.
We survive on the sea by obeying its will.
If we get too smart
And think we're the ocean's equal
We die.
It's *that* simple.
The gods are the gods and they do whatever they please,
And whatever they do is right.
Who could you appeal to against them?"

I answered, "My pride!
My defiance!
My womanhood!"

Then he gives me this shit how pride is a leaky boat,
And pats my bloating belly, and says,
"As for your womanhood, dear, it's here, and doing just fine!"
I snapped.
"Is that all I am—a brood sow for brats?"
I grabbed his prick,
"Is this all *you* are?
Is this all you want to be?"
And would you believe it?
The pig got stiff in my hand.
He just chortles away,
"It's not all that I am,
But without it, my ship has no mast!"
He laughed like a ten year old boy.
Then he asked, "Would you love me if I were a eunuch?"

I nearly said "No", but lucky for me, he kept talking.
"If you're so unhappy with this,"
—He patted my belly, again!—
"Why in God's name, did you come?
You knew this would happen.
Why didn't you let me die?
Like the poet?"

   SHE STOPS FOR A MOMENT.

An excellent question, isn't it?
What *did* happen to me?
Why didn't I let him die?
Why did I rush into slavery?

I'll tell you why—
I was raped.
Yes, *raped!*
That's how it happened.

WITH INTENSITY THAT GRADUALLY INCREASES TO HYSTERIA.

Look, here I *am* at eighteen,
Living my own private life.
Then Jason arrives and suddenly—what?
I'm head over heels in love,
Overpowered by all these feelings and urges and needs
I didn't ask for!
I lose control of my life,
Love's taken over my body, my mind, my heart . . .
Did I consent?
Of course not!
Now ask yourself—
'What is rape?'
And it's all so clear:
Rape is the act of forcing yourself on a woman—
Just like those feelings *forced* their way into my life.
So, in a way, they raped me!
Who cares if a penis ever went in or not?
I was mentally and spiritually raped.
By my own body!
By nature!
By the gods!
Jason only took over from them
—Right from the start—
With his eyes.
The first time we met, his gaze *penetrated* my soul,
He was thinking those things men *always* think about women.
I could feel them, crawling over my body

Like snakes, like worms—and then, to top it all off
Those brats he rammed into my belly—
They finished the job.
When they were born, they raped me.
From the inside out!
Twice!
Eighteen hours of sheer bloody rape!
I swear
From the day I was born, I was raped—
Raped by my father's power
And my mysogynist culture!
Raped by the simple fact of being a woman!

My life
Has been one
Long
Rape!
Mentally!
Spiritually!
Politically!
Verbally—
Yes
I've been raped by language
By words!
By thoughts!
By art!
Just look at Greek temples.
Row after row of *pillars*—
Stiff penises, *that's* what they are,
Ready for rape!
Silently threatening all women,
Warning us to submit to our roles as cows . . .

STOPS FOR A MOMENT TO COLLECT HERSELF.

When I tried to explain this to Jason
He smart-asses back, "But my dear,
You've got to admit,
It's hard to hold up a roof
With holes . . ."

When I tried to explain how trees
Were part of this patriarchal, penis-centered world,
He just laughed.
"I'm glad you see penises everywhere, dear,
It shows underneath all this shit
You're really a normal woman!"

WITH INCREASING HYSTERIA.

But he didn't stop there, oh no!
For the next little while he taunted me,
Complaining his maleness was threatened
By femininity everywhere.
Every gate, every doorway and window
Was really a hole.
Every pot, every room, every bag was a womb,
Mountains and hills were huge breasts,
And finally, to make me go mad
He said tunnels were penises in reverse,
And, so in a way, I had a penis
Which sort of hung inward!

*A LONG PAUSE AS SHE PULLS HERSELF TOGETHER
AGAIN.*

His plan to drive me insane didn't work.
It just made me realize
My marriage was also a war.

Sex was a total invasion of privacy,
An attack on my sacred space!
I was a conquered country.
And that's when it hit me—
What I need is *power!*
To repel the invader,
To take back my life,
To counter-attack
And destroy the enemy!
Power,
That was the answer!
Nothing else matters.
Not truth.
Not love.
Not goodness or beauty.
Just power.

Any lie is good
If it gives me more power.
Any ugliness becomes beautiful
If it gives me power.
Any crime, any vice, is a virtue
If it gets me more power!
And truth that denies my power
Is evil!
It cannot be true
And I will destroy
Those who say different!
Silence
—Except for the sound of my voice—
Will be the sign of my triumph!

These thoughts poured into my mind like cool, clear rain,
Beautiful, simple answers to all my problems.
And I knew just how to begin.
I declared war on nature,
Collaborator with men and betrayer of women.

From that day onward, only *my* thoughts,
My ideas, *my* beliefs and *my* wishes counted.
I ignored, I trampled whatever was 'natural'.
Dozens of times a day, I said to myself,
"I shit on nature, I shit on love, I shit on men,
I shit on motherhood and happy slave women!"

And to hell with the gods!
I declared myself my own goddess.

As much as I could, I avoided anything male.
Jason, of course, well, what could I do?
If I didn't let him rape me he'd beat me to death.
But I made it unpleasant.
And, let me tell you,
I aborted six of his brats in the shit-house.
I laughed whenever he took a dump on his bastards.

And as for the twins
No mother-slavery for me!
They went to a nurse, who kept them most of the day.
"Raise them like girls," I said, and when the dumb cow
Looked at me like I was crazy I slapped her.
"Should they grow up to be rapists, just like their father?"
If she didn't obey
I told her I'd shrivel her breasts and stop her bleeding!
She was so frightened of being free, she obeyed.

In the mean time, I looked for new ways to get power . . .

Fortunately, at this time we arrived in Iolcus.
Now that he had the fleece
Jason could get back the throne
From the uncle of his
Who stole it when Jason was born.

But there was a problem:
Pelias, you see, was a popular king,
So Jason couldn't charge in
And just hack him to pieces . . .

Good thing I had a plan.

I went to the palace disguised as an ancient crone,
So ugly no man would look at me twice
And begged to talk to the daughters.
I had a miracle for the old king.

SHE RE-ENACTS THE SCENE.

When they arrived, I showed them.
I cut a ram into pieces and dumped him into a pot.
And I sang these 'magical' words—just gibberish, really,
When lo and behold, a frisky young ram jumps out
And runs from the palace.
The trick is quite simple.
I learned it when I was twelve—
But they fall for it every time.

I said I could do the same for Pelias,
That way the old man could rule them forever.
These girls were amazed.
They rushed to give him the news
And soon he arrives, an old stick,
Propped up by two other sticks.
When *he* sees the magic,
His eyes pop out of his head!
He couldn't wait to get started,
So I gave him a sleeping potion and when he was down
I handed the knives to his daughters.
"The honor belongs to you."
They looked kind of sick

But, being good daughters
—Good slaves—
They got down to work.
And you should have seen them!
Bloody from head to toe,
Right up to their elbows in gore,
Chopping and slicing,
Believing the smaller they cut him
The younger he'd be . . .

You know, they were almost like children,
Tossing his tripes in the pot
And sloshing around in his guts.
They felt
A kind of hysterical, desperate happiness.
But, you know, I believe
They were also secretly pleased with themselves,
Drunk with the pleasure of killing a man,
Especially a father . . .

And then, it was time.
They looked at me, hardly breathing,
Their faces so wretchedly hopeful,
Pathetic, and helpless,
And suddenly . . . so afraid . . .

You know what I said?

"Congratulations!
There's one less man in the world!
Now go all the way and proclaim yourselves queens of Iolcus!
Be women of power!
Free our sisters!
Raise a republic of women!
I'll use my magic to help you!"

And what did *they* do?
They babbled and blubbered,
Weeping, screaming, begging for me
To save their *dear* father.
I wasn't afraid of these ninnies.
I slapped them a couple of times,
Good and hard.
They needed it bad.
"Be women! Be strong!"
But they cried even more,
Whimpering, 'O the gods this' and 'O the gods that.'
Useless tits, cowards, traitors . . .
So I just walked out of the palace,
I didn't care—
It was *their* problem.
They did the killing, not me.

Thanks to them, the whole thing was a mess.
The King's Council debated our case and said things were even:
Jason had his revenge for losing the throne
But, he would never be king.
And I would never, *ever* be queen.

Hell, they were rioting in the streets.
Mobs screaming. "Pelias! Pelias!"
They wanted to hang his daughters,
They wanted to tear me apart and burn the Argo
So Jason and I had to flee—
To Corinth.

SHE STOPS TO REFLECT.

Now, I admit, I'm a lousy loser.
Women have been good losers for way too long,
And having lost in Iolcus I made up my mind,
At least I would win at home.

More than ever
I turned my marriage
Into a power-play.
I didn't care how.
Truth, lies, slander—whatever it took.
My life was a show of force.
It was war.
Once, twice, three times a day
I lectured Jason about the oppression of women
And how every man
Must *personally* pay for those crimes.

Jason, of course, didn't get it.
"I owe you nothing for other men's crimes.
I didn't commit them, and *you* weren't the victim,
So why the hell should I pay you?"

I told him, "The personal *is* the political.
Whether you know it or not,
You're an accomplice in every crime against women.
Merely by being a man
You've profited from those crimes.
Thus, you *are* guilty and thus *you* must pay,
Personally—in your case, to me."

The truth is
All men are born guilty,
And all deserve to be punished.

They have oppressed us women so much
Offending, disturbing a woman in any way whatsoever
Is criminal.
A man is guilty—*if* charged!
That's our new feminist justice.

And for once he had nothing to say,
No laugh, no smirk, no smart answer,
He just gave me this look like he's never seen me before . . .

And you know what he does?

Instead of admitting I'm right, he walks out the door.
He goes back to live on the Argo along with his men . . .
He's not coming back, he tells me.

So there I am, a poor, helpless mother,
Stuck with two little children
And nobody to support me.

And then?
You guessed it!
He finds a bimbo,
Some breathless dumb slut
All eager to understand him and patch up his wounds,
And betray her sisters for fun in the sack and some brats . . .

And you know who the little slut was?
Glauce.
King Creon's daughter.
Marriage to *her*
Makes Jason the king of Corinth
When Creon dies!

When I heard that, I went ballistic.
Jason, the King of Corinth?
That city used to belong to *my* family,
And therefore was *mine* by natural right,
Not hers, and not by the Goddess,
Not his!
I—I should be queen of Corinth!

Why should he marry some hot little bitch
And make himself king, while I have to slave for my bread,
Selling potions to love-sick girls and giddy old matrons?
Already I could hear them bleating,
"Baaa, baaaaa . . . relaaaaaaaationship,
Maaaaaan, husbaaaaand, baaaaabies . . ."
Mush-headed sheep!
They'd be happier if I cut off their heads
And gave them another cunt!

But I wasn't taking this shit lying down.
I went straight to the palace to see this Glauce,
And straighten her out about Jason and men
And the sisterhood of all women.

*SHE RE-ENACTS GLAUCE'S SPEECHES TO SATIRIZE HER
AS A 'BIMBO'.*

"Welcome, Medea," she says,
"And don't worry.
You can *depend* on me
To look after you and your children.
Whatever you need, just ask.
I'll personally see you get it!"

I know a bitch when I see one!
"I don't need you—or anyone else!" I snarled.

She gives me this sweet poison smile,
"I know how you feel.
Freedom and independence are worth any price—
Even *poverty.*
Bread-crusts and rags aren't much,
But at least they're your own—
And you're free . . ."

She knew how to rub in the salt.
But I got straight to my point.
"Your majesty, I have come
To share a glorious plan,
A plan to free women
From enslavement to gods
And nature,
And men!
You, with your power and I, with my knowledge,
Will build a nation ruled for the good of all women,
A world where women are free to be only themselves
And free from the lies of love and the evils of maleness—
A world without men!"

She smiled at me like you smile at a fool.
"No men?
But I need regular fucking
Or else I turn into a bitch!
And besides,
How do we get more women?"

"We can adopt them," I said, "from other cities."
She frowned,
So I told her we'll keep a few studs for breeding
And trade the boy-brats for girls.

"You're crazy," she laughs.
"Who wants to breed with a slave?
I'm not a cow!
I'm a woman,
I want to fuck with my man."
She giggled.
"Sex with a slave is like riding a plough-horse—

Safe, but not too exciting.
I'd rather ride thorough-breds.
More dangerous, yes,
But if you know how to handle them
Lots more fun."

Then she looks at me with her dolly-girl eyes.
"You never learned men-handling, did you?
I'll teach you myself, if you like—
I know!
Let's make a deal—
You teach me moon-magic,
And I'll teach you men-magic!"

I shut up but she thought I agreed
And rode her mouth off at a gallop.
"This story," she says, "is the basis of all men-magic.
My grandmother taught me when I was a little girl,
About the pot and the spoon.

You see, the pot once said to herself,
'Why do I need the stirring spoon?
Why should I share the glory?
I carry the food and *I* sit on the fire,
All the spoon does is dive in.'

So the pot tries to cook by herself.
And you can imagine,
Dinners were terrible.
Everything burned,
And the pot was nearly thrown out.
But this little pot wasn't dumb.
She soon figured out that things needed stirring up,
And that's where the spoon came in.

Of course, the spoon discovered
By itself, it was only a stick.
Useful in simple ways but not a lot more . . .

So the cooking pot and the stirring spoon
Did the only sensible thing—
They fell in love.
They accepted themselves
—And each other—
Just as they were,
And doing what they did best
Together they made good pudding . . ."

I told her I didn't give a fuck about cooking,
And the little snot says, "I know.
That's why you're missing a spoon."
Dumb broad!
What did she think we were—
Cats fighting over a tom?

"I'm not here about Jason!" I said,
And she smiles, all pity and poison.
"I hear you—but don't believe you,"
And lays her hand on my shoulder as if she's comforting me.
"Medea, it's not the end of the world.
There *are* other men,
Only next time remember
Something my horse-trainer told me,
'Many a beast that can't be broken, *can* be gentled.'"

Gentled!
Is she using shit for brains?
We're
Supposed to gentle *them?*
Have they ever gentled *us?*

O sure—
If rape is gentle,
Raping us all the time,
And not just with penises—
But looking and leering.
And thinking those thoughts
And beating us too, night and day
Forever punching and kicking.

And little Miss Sunshine gives me a standing ovation,
Clapping like crazy, "Wow, what an act!
You should take it on stage!
If I didn't know better,
I'd swear you believed it yourself!"
I told her I did, and her eyes got this big,

"Really?"

By the Great Mother, how naïve can you get?

"Get into the real world,
See for yourself how they treat us."
And she, this little Miss Dozy, tells me,
"I know. It's terrible.
People aren't nice to each other.
Not men—
And not women either.
Women are mean with words,
They go straight for the heart.
And they're violent too.
I've seen them scratching and biting.
And shoving and kicking and throwing things.
But then, of course, you, of all people,
Know women can be as violent as men—
Don't you?"

Bitch!
What choice did I have in killing my brother or Pelias?
Women have been disempowered so long
We *have* to go to extremes to get what's rightfully ours.
It's *that* simple.
But this happy slave,
This spoiled little princess
Who's spent her whole life in a palace
Doesn't know a slap from a woman
Is not like a slap from a man.
We've been oppressed,
So we need to lash out
To regain our freedom.
Violence is therapeutic for us
But men don't need to hit back.

Our happy slave, of course, can't see it that way.
"Let me show you my grandmother's lesson."

She calls and this wolf-dog comes running,
Teeth like daggers and drooling like rain.
"Down," she says, and he flops to the floor.
"He's a wonderful dog," she gushes,
Then orders the guard to hand me a spear.
"Give him a poke in the ribs—
With the blunt end, of course."

I do, but the mutt just ignores it.
"Poke him again," she says.
One eye pops open. "Again."
And now this monster looks up.
He's thinking, 'Play—or attack?'

The next time she asked, I refused.
"He'll bite me," I said,
And she rolls her baby blue eyes and cries out,
"But why?
You didn't bite *him*!
But you're lucky, I'm letting you off.
My grandmother made me poke him
Until he growled and showed me his teeth.
Then she said, 'Remember this, Glauce.
It's something most women forget:
A lot of small pokes
Sooner or later add up
To a great big bite!' "

I should have known better, of course.
But . . . I tried . . .
Patience and kindness to fools
Have always been one of my weak points.

I explained how right from the start
Men oppressed women.
But she wouldn't even listen.
She said I was blowing it out of proportion.
Oh, she agreed, life wasn't perfect for women,
But nothing like what I said,
Systematic, intentional
Planned oppression
Driven by hatred for women.
She laughed in my face.
"You're giving them too much credit!
Men aren't *that* smart—or well organized.
The moment they get a hard-on
Most of their brains go dead!"

And then she got mad.
My views were an insult to women.
I was insulting all our foremothers
Right back to the dawn of time
Because—now get this—she says,
"If women were fooled and enslaved for so long
Doesn't it kind of prove
We really *are* stupid and weak?
If we didn't catch on
Until *you* arrived to enlighten us all
Then we *must* be inferior!
Either that—
Or your theory is, well, full of shit."

That's when I knew there wasn't a hope for that girl.
She didn't want to be saved.
She was a natural fool and the sad thing is,
Fools have to burn so the rest of the world can see.
It's war:
Some die
So others can live.

I thanked her,
Humbly bowing and scraping,
I asked her permission to leave.
She promised again to care of me and the brats,
And said next time she wanted to learn some moon-magic.
I promised to show her a really fabulous trick,
One that she'd never forget . . .

And I did.
Oh yes, I did . . .

For a wedding gift, I sewed her a beautiful cloak,
Red and gold silk, with embroidered flowers and birds,
And a happy couple walking beside the sea.

They didn't have silk in Greece, so I knew she'd love it
And put it on right away.
She'd never resist that mystical shimmering gold
And that passionate red which I made with the blood of an owl.

It was so beautiful
For a moment *I* wanted to wear it,
To see myself in a mirror
Shimmering like a goddess.
I heard the silk whispering,
'Wear me! Wear me, and be divine!'
What bride could say no?
What women does not want divinity?

And just as I knew she would,
At her wedding she put it on,
And started dancing for Jason . . .

That's when the moon-magic started!
Suddenly, the robe burst into flame!
Pure, white hot flame!
The magical fire of moonlight
Licked out of the collar and sleeves,
Fusing her back and her breasts
And her legs and her crotch to the silk.
The gown stuck to her skin
Setting her flesh on fire!

SPEAKS AS IF RE-LIVING THE SCENE.

Ah, Glauce, you bitch
Now you're really in heat,
So dance—
Dance for your husband!
She him how heat makes you twist
Like a flame in the wind.

Ah yes—*yes*!
I see you thrashing,
I hear you screaming,
Your breasts are on fire,
Your tender nipples are burning.
Show it all to him, Glauce,
Open your legs, you shameless bitch,
And show him the fire licking your cunt!

It's my fire,
My fire makes you this hot!
Do you think he's jealous
Of how my fire can make you squirm?
Ah, but where *is* your husband, Glauce ?
Where's Jason?
Isn't he coming to save you?

He's smarter than you.
He knows if he touches you once
He'll start to burn!
Anyone touching you will burst into flame!

He's standing there, watching you die, Glauce.
No hero-death,
No romantic love-death for him.
He'll live without you, my dear,
As he learned to live without me.

But don't worry, he won't be lonely.
Already the sluts are buzzing around his door,
Like blow-flies Glauce, buzzing around your body—

*LAUGHS HYSTERICALLY, THEN SUDDENLY COLLAPSES
TO THE FLOOR.*

Oh weep for womanhood, Glauce.
Cry, weep, despair,
For as long as there are men
Womanhood is a house divided against itself.

Only hatred can free us, Glauce—
Women must fall in hate
Or end up like you, my beautiful sister,
My beautiful burning symbol
Of womankind's self-destruction!

O Glauce, you burn for the greater glory of women!
How else could I save you from him
And the tyranny of your nature?
My martyr! My saint!
Remember, it's really Jason who set you on fire!
It is I who have given you freedom,
And strength, O sister, and peace—
Yes! I am giving you peace!
For what else is peace to a woman
But freedom from men?

Ah, my dear Glauce, already I see
Forgiveness in your sweet eyes.
I know your heart understands
And loves me for what I have done—
Farewell, my sweet daughter,
Until we embrace in the heavens!

VEHEMENTLY, AS IF JASON WERE PRESENT.

Jason, you dog! You coward!
You watched her die!
You stood there and let your woman die for you,
You—*man!*

Where's all that hero stuff, big-boy?
Don't feel like dying today?
Not ready to be a legend?
No statues for you just yet?

But a woman's not worth it, is she?
There's always more where she came from,
Lots of hot sluts just dying to crawl to your bed.

But what's that look on your face?
Ah, Jason, suddenly you remember—
Your sons!
What have I done to your dear, precious sons?
Do you want to know?
And why are you suddenly running, Jason?
Running
—As never before—
Run little boy!
Run!

EXULTANTLY.

Too late—toooo late!
They're already dead!
While you were watching your new bride dance,
I slit their throats.
I sacrificed them like rams to our mother the moon!
I drained their blood into the streets!
A couple of pigs are licking it up
And they're grunting with pleasure!

And I want you to know, they begged for their lives—
Your sons
Begged for their lives!
When they saw the knife, they screamed,
"Please Mommy, no!"

They didn't fight—
They *begged!*
Like slaves!
Like whipped dogs!
Your sons, Jason—
Your sons!

And they called for you, Jason,
But you weren't there.
You were watching your new bride dance!
And you know what you'll find when you get home, Jason?
Me—on a chariot!
And my feet will be resting
On the soft, white flesh of your sons!
They're softer than pillows
And warmer than brass!
I win, Jason.
I win and through me
All womankind wins . . .

My chariot is drawn by three dragons,
Past, present and future.
Do you know what that means, Jason?
Do you know what that means?

It means this story will never end.
I'll fight for womanhood age after age,
Until we're victorious!
Until women are free!
Free
From slavery to love!
Free
From slavery to nature!
Free
From the chains of our bodies!
And free
From that sickness called men!

I'm fighting you now, Jason.
Right here on this stage.
This woman-sister, this actress, has lent me her body
So my spirit can speak and wage war against you.
And not only you, but war against maleness.

I'm winning, Jason!
I'm winning
My plan is successful even beyond *my* dreams!

*SUDDENLY SNAPS BACK INTO THE PRESENT. SHE SPEAKS
DIRECTLY TO AUDIENCE.*

You know why?
'Cause *I've*
Got the hydrogen bomb of the gender wars,
The ultimate weapon to blast men out of control
And put women in charge forever!
And that weapon is—
Sensitive new age guys!

And it's all so simple!
If we can't clip men between the legs,
Clip them between the ears.
If we can't clip their balls, clip their brains!

Turn them all into sensitive new age guys,
Profoundly sorry,
Embarrassed for being born men,
Ashamed of having testosterone,
Ashamed of . . . anything male.

We've got these guys convinced
That a baby boy
Is only a broken girl
And needs to be fixed!

They are the source of all evil!
Male-kind's only achievement
Has been the enslavement of women!
Each invention, each book or painting,
Was possible only because
A man couldn't rape a woman,
And so all his semen spurted up into his brain
And came out as something else!

These new, ashamed men
All want to play Jesus Christ,
And take on themselves
The sins of their fathers!
And we new women
Will make their wishes come true!
We'll turn their lives
Into one
Long crucifixion!

Before we're done with these boys
They'll be wanting their periods!
And maybe, some day they'll have them,
And babies too!

Then women—at last—will be free
To be our true feminine selves!
Free from our slavery to cunts,
Unchained from our tits and wombs!
Then our womanly nature will show its true self at last
And a female civilization will blossom!

Is this not revenge worth waiting for?
Is this not a beautiful vision?
Millions of shriveled penises,
Millions—no, billions—of shrunken balls,
And shrunken heads!

Every man will spend his whole life
Dying to be a girl.
And whenever we want to put a man in his place,
We'll just hiss, 'Man!'
And he'll cringe!
He'll *beg* to be punished again
—By you!—
For the crime of being born male!

O sisters, I tell you, this new matriarchal order
Is only moments away,
And *I* will lead you to victory,
Not as your queen,
Not like some patriarchal ruler—
Oh no!
But as your Big Sister,
Watching you,
Shielding you from your moments of weakness.

I know that many of you have your special man.
'He's different,' you say,
'He's not like the others,
He's the exception.'

But I, your Big Sister, will gently remind you,
He's a man, and it's only a dream.
All men are the same and one moment of weakness for him
Weakens all women.
One moment of weakness, no matter how sweet it seems,
Is treason against yourself and your sisters!

Give me, your Big Sister, the burden of knowing these things.
Trust me to guide your thinking, your feelings, your speech
Into the proper womanly channels.
Let me, little sisters, look after your happiness . . .

And now my dear little sisters, I have spoken enough.
Thanks to this dear, dear girl who lent her flesh to my spirit,
You know my true story.
Through her I have spoken across the ages and refuted the lies
That I was a heartless, power-mad monster,
For like you, I was only a victim,
Always, always a victim . . .

And so I ask you to join me,
Fall into love with woman,
And fall into hate with men.
Join me in battle.
Be one of Medea's Bitches
And advance for the glory of women!

LIGHTS OUT

JASON

A BASEMENT REC ROOM: A SMALL PATIO TABLE AND CHAIR, SOME WEIGHTS, A FEW HUNTING TROPHIES ON THE WALL ALONG WITH A FEW GREEK TRAVEL POSTERS AND PERHAPS PICTURES OF A FEW WARSHIPS. JASON, IN BLACK SLACKS AND T-SHIRT (OR TURTLE-NECK) SITS AT THE TABLE, CLEANING A RIFLE, SEEMINGLY ABSORBED IN THIS TASK. THERE ARE PILES OF BOOKS AND MAGAZINES ON THE TABLE, CHAIRS, FLOOR AROUND HIM. HE MUST GIVE THE IMPRESSION OF 'OFFICER MATERIAL'. THE IMPRESSION OF 'POTENTIAL VIOLENCE', OR A VIOLENT PAST, MUST REMAIN THROUGHOUT THE PLAY. ONCE THE AUDIENCE HAS SETTLED IN, HE LOOKS UP, PUTS A LAST FEW FINISHING BUFFS ON THE RIFLE, AND, AFTER CAREFULLY, LAYING DOWN THE RIFLE, HE GETS UP, BRIEFLY SURVEYS THE AUDIENCE, AND STARTS.

So, you want the truth?
About me—Jason,
The Argonaut,
World-famous hero,
The man who ripped off the Golden Fleece—
And not just the Fleece.
I stole the King's daughter too—
Right from under his nose,
And she butchered her own little brother
To celebrate the occasion . . .

The truth about me is simple—
Real simple:
I
Am a hunter.
A killer.

Want to know something else?

Every man is.

Every man,
From the moment the Y sperm
Punctures his mother's egg,
Is a hunter, a killer,
Right 'til the day he dies.

And that's the glory
—And sorrow—
Of being a man.

The glory because it means
The world is
—And forever will be—
A *man's* world.

When the shit hits the fan,
When that thin little layer
Of what we call 'civilization'
Is ripped down by some kind of disaster,
When earthquakes hit,
And the power's out
And machines don't work
And the stores are all empty,
And all that's left is the natural world

Of eat or be eaten,
When 'progress' means nothing
But being alive in the morning,
Women will always need
—And call for—
A man.
A hunter,
A killer,
To fix
And feed
And protect.

And that's our sorrow:
Men do the dirty work,
Hunting and butchering,
Lifting and lugging,
Killing and dying,
So women and children can live . . .

That's it.
That's the natural world.
That's how it's been for millions of years.
And nothing can stop it
No matter how much we try . . .

DISMISSIVELY, AS IF TO AN UNHEARD OBJECTION.

Yeah yeah, I know,
We can pass laws,
And write up bills of equality.
Hell, we can have thousands of bright ideas
But ask yourself just one thing:
Is Nature listening?
Do you really think Nature
Gives a goddamn what we think?

Will Nature change because humans wrote up some law?

*PAUSES TO LET THE ANSWER TO THIS RHETORICAL
QUESTION SINK IN.*

Those are the plain, simple facts,
And Medea
—And *every* woman—
Better accept them now.
Nature won't change,
And the men in their lives,
Their brothers and boyfriends and lovers,
Their husbands and sons
Are hunters
—And killers—
Like me.

The truth is, a man's heart
Lives for hunting.
The sweetest taste to his soul
Is the orgasm—of *victory!*
Of a kill brought down,
And a trophy dragged home.

The only difference in men
Is in *what* they hunt.

Some men
Only hunt meat—
Animals, enemies, women . . .

Others hunt danger,
Or fame, or power, or wealth . . .

A few
Hunt beauty, or justice, or knowledge . . .

And finally, the rarest of all,
Those who hunt God . . .

But the bottom line is
Every man,
Every *real* man,
Hunts something.
And when he stops hunting,
There's nothing left but a corpse
That just happens to breathe.

Men who don't hunt anymore
Are zombies.
Dead men,
Pretending to live,
And women who live with such men
Are sleeping with corpses.

CHUCKLES MALICIOUSLY FOR A FEW MOMENTS.

You know, it's a very rare marriage
That isn't a liar's club.
Mine was . . .

Medea
—Like most women—
Wasn't ready to hear the truth about men,
Or about women either . . .

Imagine—Medea,
Moon-priestess, world famous witch,
Expert on all things female,
Silly enough to believe
She could ever be first
In a real man's life!

She asks me
—She *actually* asks—

MIMICS HER IN A MOCKING WAY AS HE WILL DO WHEN-EVER HE QUOTES HER.

"Jason, are you saying I'm *not*
The most important thing in your life?"

AS IF ACTUALLY TALKING TO HER AGAIN FOR A MOMENT.

"For God's sake, Medea,
Haven't you ever seen sperm?
What do they do?
They move!
They fight!
They're after something!
That's what men do!
That's what men *are*!

Men who don't hunt or fight or move forward,
Are dead.
Men—and sperm—are like salmon:
Only the dead ones go with the flow!"

Then I made the *only* mistake of my life:
I told a woman the truth
About her and me

"*You* are the most important
Thing that I *chose*.
But I didn't choose
To be born a man
So *first* of all, I'm a hunter."

Then she asks, "Well Jason, tell me,
Where *do* I fit into your life?"

And, having been stupid once,
I'm stupid again!
"You are my first
—And best—
Hunting partner . . ."

And that's how it started between us.
The truth wasn't good enough for Medea.
Like every women
She wanted to be
More than a hunting partner.
She wanted to be
My goddess.

You can see it right in their bodies.
There's the egg,
Like a queen on her little throne,
Surrounded by sperm,
Millions of courtiers whose only desire,
Whose only purpose for being
Is to fight and die for the honor
Of being the first . . .

She drops little hints,
Waves this one away,
Calls that one closer,
Lets them all wait in suspense,
Holds them all in her power,
Inspecting, rejecting and finally, accepting
The one who has what *she* wants—
No matter how stupid it is.

Ever look at a peacock?
Don't they have beautiful tails?
And pea-hens just love them!
The bigger, the better!
They screw the guys with big tails.

You know what else that tail is?
A death warrant!
Calling to every predator
"Eat me, I'm slow
'Cause I'm dragging this mop."
Does the pea-hen care?
Not on your life!
She just wants sperm
From a guy with a big heavy tail.

So that's what guys deliver . . .

Peacocks or human,
Guys are poor fools.
Big tails, or big cars,
Big horns, or big paychecks,
Whatever the females want

Guys have to deliver the goods,
Even if it kills them.
And, if they don't—
They don't fuck,
So their genes die out.

Either way, guys lose.

Guys
Are expendable.

PAUSES TO LET THIS SINK IN.

Now, if it wasn't so dumb
I'd be like Medea.
I'd scream how much Nature hates guys,
And how it's so bloody unfair.
But you know something else?
So fucking what?
Nature
—What they used to call 'the gods'—
Couldn't care less!
Nature's got other
—*And way bigger*—
Fish to fry
Than meeting *our* expectations.

So, guys,
Don't bother raising a stink.
It won't change a thing.
Nature is like the sea:
You accept it for better or worse
And take every advantage you can.
That's it.
Simple and straight,
Just like a good man's prick!

SURVEYS AUDIENCE; THEN, AS IF GUESSING A SECRET.

I know what you're thinking—
"Where's 'love' in this picture?
Is it just eggs and sperm?"

Of course not—
No more than a boat
Is nothing but sail.
But like it or not,
That egg and sperm stuff
Is the wind pushing the boat.

I know about love.
I'm as 'lovey' as anyone else,
But I know what motivates love.
Flowers and dinners and dancing
All lead to one thing—
And sure, that's a blast,
But it's got a serious plot:
If *he* doesn't plant his genes
They don't make the next generation,
And *she* needs quality sperm
And a good, reliable butler for her and the brats.

And when he arrives,
The butler,
The *quality* prick with its *quality* sperm,
All ready and eager to worship
The egg on its throne,
She, like a gracious goddess
Consents to be conquered . . .

That's what love is to women—
Being worshipped and served by a man.
They yearn for it, 24/7
365 . . .

And you know where the proof is?
Right in the cash box!
Half the books sold each day
Are *romance* novels!
Half of what this whole planet
Reads every day,
Year after year,
Is all about one thing only:
Being adored,
And served
—And serviced—
By the right man!

Look at the women's mags at your supermarket!
What are they mostly about?
Getting, and keeping, a guy.

That's what most women want,
Not that feminist crap.
They know if you stick your nose
Into *Ms* for too long
You'll be looking down
When your pool boy walks by
And then—no cabana!

That's what men are to women
—Pool boys—
Though guys try fooling themselves
Into thinking they're 'knights',
Shining armor and all that shit . . .

Ha!
Listen up guys—
You're pool boys,
Or food for the old black widow.

Of course, I've got to admit,
Wanting to be adored
Is their weakness too!
Convince her you have no wish
Except worshipping her
And she'll let you into her shrine.

CHUCKLES AND CONTINUES TRIUMPHANTLY.

And don't they fall for those lines
Age, after age, after age?

And what happens next?
He leaves her in search of new targets,
Or thinks about something else.

They're so damn easy to fool!
All you need is—
Words.

They love those golden-tongued bastards
Who know how to talk.

Medea was no exception.
She had this 'poet'.

You know what a 'poet' is to a woman?
Any guy who can *talk* his way up her skirt.

This 'poet' came for the fleece,
And believe it or not,
Medea was *dying* to help him.
She actually *begged* him
To take the moon oil
And all of her magical potions.

The stupid bugger refuses.
He thought his voice and his verses
Could get him the fleece . . .
Yeah right,
Verses—against a dragon!
He should have stuck to the fleeces
Between women's legs.

And that's what I can't figure out.
Whenever she talked about him
Her eyes got all glassy.
Her great "might have been love" she called him,
My "only rival."

PAUSES IN DISBELIEF.

My rival—a poet?

She had to be kidding.
You can't kill dragons with poems,
Or look after women and kids . . .
And she smiled, goddamnit!
She was *always* smiling at me
Like I was a kid or something,
A snot-nosed brat—
And she'd say,
"What's the matter, Jason?
Jealous?"

Yeah, sure, I'm jealous all right,
Of some guy who sings for his supper
Instead of dragging it home.
"Poems don't feed you," I told her
And she always said, "You're right.
Food keeps you alive
But poems make you *want* to keep living.
That's worth something too,
And *that's* where the poets come in . . ."

"Oh for God's sake,
A poet is just a guy
With the words to get up your skirt."
And she'd smile again
—That 'womanly mystery' smile—
That makes men feel like such fools,
And she'd say, "Maybe—
But maybe not.
And who cares?
The fact is, they get there.
Shouldn't that tell you something?"

It sure as hell does—
Women
Like being lied to.
Sure they complain about it—
And then they reward the liars.

But what about guys like me—
Plain, simple guys
Who tell them the truth?

Then she starts laughing again,
Right in my face,
And talks like I was a kid.

"Jason, when will you learn
That truth may be true—
But it's not always true enough?"

What's that supposed to mean,
"True, but not true enough."?
It's true or it's not, right?
And she'd give me this lecture
—Wasn't she always?—
"Truth must be true,
But in the right way for the listener,
And in the right time and place."

So I asked her,
"If plain simple truth isn't good enough,
Why didn't you run off with him?"

You know what she says?
"I would have—
But he was *stupid.*
Self-made stupid,
Like you!
So proud!
So damn independent!
He rejected my help
'Cause he thought
—Just like a man—
He could do it all by himself.
He figured that *he*
Had all the right tools."

She told me not to forget
I wouldn't have gotten the fleece
Without her and her magic.

Bullshit!
I would have found a way.
I'm Jason,
The hunter, the killer,
I always get what I'm after.

She waved me off when I said that.
She didn't have an answer
Against the truth . . .

SHAKES HIS HEAD AND SIGHS WITH EXASPERATION.

You know, I thought she'd be happy
Not to be number one in my life!
That way she's *free*!
She'll have all that independence
She's always talking about.

Instead, she wallows in tears,
"How could I *ever* have loved you?"

She loved me because she saw
What *all* women want in a man
—The same thing they look for in horses—
A winner!

You know how they spot a winner?
By the lines,
By the aura,
And the feeling of danger.
Their four million year old genes
Look for a hunter, a killer,
A guy who can feed and protect . . .

CHUCKLES.

'What do you do for a living?'
Really means, 'How well can you hunt
For me and our kids?'

Ah yes, the sight of a winner
Makes their hearts go aflutter.
Like I did.
I strutted up to her father
And bowed—a little—and said,
"Aetes, my name is Jason,
I've come for the Golden Fleece!"
As if it was only a parcel
Instead of the greatest,
Most dangerous prize in the world.

Sheer bluff, of course.
I didn't know squat!
I had nothing but balls—
And a hunter's belief
If I make the right noise,
I'll flush something out of the bush.

And I did.

As I looked through the crowd, I saw her,
Staring at me
With bright, hungry eyes.
Any man would have noticed.

She stood near the throne,
And others, except an old nurse,
Kept a respectful distance.
I knew in a flash:

A princess!
Most likely Aetes' daughter,
Who likes what she sees . . .

I smiled at her quickly—a signal,
'I've seen you', and said,
As flippantly as I dared,
"Your majesty, when may I get it?"

He darkened with rage.
I saw how she smiled even more.
Aha!
She liked my defiance!
She was fed up with fathers
And wanted a lover.
I knew right away
I had a friend in the palace.

"Get?" roars Aetes,
"Did you just say 'get it', you boy?
Hundreds have died for it, bastard,
Men better and smarter than you,
Roasted and eaten alive by man-eating oxen,
Shredded like fruit in the teeth of a sleepless dragon,
Slowly chewed over, like cud.
And that's what you'll 'get'—if you're lucky,
You impudent piece of pig-shit!
But maybe I'll fry you alive,
And repeat your words to you, boy,
As my dogs eat the guts I'll yank from your living belly . . ."

I saw her face darken with fear—
She was already worried for me!
I looked at her hard
And sent a thought through my eyes,
'Will you help?'

And the answer came back in a flash
'Yes! Wait!'
She suddenly left the room.
And I started to play for more time.

I bowed and scraped to Aetes.
"Your majesty, please forgive my plain soldier's talk,
I assure you, great King,
My men and I have no plans
But awaiting your majesty's pleasure."

That son-of-a-bitch was no fool.
He knew right away I was different.
Under my ass-kissing talk
He heard me laughing.

He gives me this quizzical look,
Trying to guess my secret,
Then waves me away . . .

He let us wait a few days
Watching our preparations.
He didn't see much.

I was making them all at night.
In bed—with his daughter.

Later she'd tell other women,
"He enslaved me right from the start!
I offered to help and he—raped me!
The very first night!"

Yeah, right . . .

The truth is, she saw her winner
And did what it took to get him.

A little dive in the sack
Was a small price to pay.

RE-ENACTING THE CONVERSATION.

Later she'd say,
"How dare you?"
How dare you portray me like that?"

"You didn't select me?
You didn't smile,
Your eyes didn't promise
Wide-open bed-room doors?

You enslaved yourself!
You came 'cause you saw a winner!
And when a woman sees that,
There's nothing—
Nothing at all she won't do!
No deed is too low, no crime too horrendous,
Not when her unborn children
Are crying for life in her womb!
You're the living proof, baby!
You sold out your family,
Your country,
You moon-priestess vows,
You killed your brother—
For what?
Your kids from the right pair of balls!"

"Oh! And to think I gave up everything for you . . ."

"Bull shit!
You gave up *nothing* that mattered to you any more!
Moon-oils and crystals and magical charms were *nothing*
Compared to the magical liquid I brewed in my balls!

Goddamn it, for once face the truth!
You were finished with games
And ready to do a woman's *real* work—
Bringing life to this world!"

Oh God, did she lose it then . . .

    CHUCKLES.

Anyway, after a week
Aetes gave me the call to try for the fleece.
You know the rest.
I swiped it.

With her help, of course.
But the fact is, I, being a man,
Did all the dirty work,
Took *all* the chances.
If I failed,
Well, sad but too bad,
She'd wait for another boat—
And another guy.

Now, don't get me wrong:
I don't blame her.
She was a woman,
With a future family to think of,
Things more important than me
Or any particular guy.
So, it had to be me in the natural male position—
The fall guy, who takes the chances.

But you know, I didn't mind.
I'm a natural guy, so I know
Men are always covering women,
In bed—or in danger.

That's the way Nature made us.

And wants us to stay that way too,
The covering and the covered,
Working together
For the good of our kind . . .

Medea, of course, doesn't give a cold fuck about Nature.
She's a sorceress, a technician.
She only wants to impose her will on Nature,
And kick Nature's ass.

Of course, she forgets
Mother Nature
Is the original bitch.
Sooner or later
Nature
Kicks back.

She should have learned that on Lemnos.

Lemnos, if you ever knew,
Is an island in the Aegean.
We landed there soon after stealing
The Golden Fleece.

What a mess!
Husbands and wives had been fighting,
So the men got new girls.
The wives, pretending they're sorry,
Get the men back into bed
And finished them off—

You know what?
Good for the girls!
Sounds brutal, but listen.
These guys were polluting the gene-pool!
They were too stupid to see
No wife wants her ex in the sack
Unless she's got something planned.

These clowns were too proud of their pricks!
They figure the old lady's crazy
For another taste of the best
And so, waving their joy sticks they run—
Right into their graves!
God!
Men can be such damn fools!

And then—get this—the old hens
Set up a women's republic.
First, of course, they give the new chicks
A sisterly boot in the ass
And from that day on
They live in this 'ideal' feminist state,
Ruled *by* women,
For the good of all women.
No men allowed, and none wanted.
Just dildo's,
And sisterly fingers and tongues . . .

After five years of this perfect women's republic
What did they learn?

Don't fuck with Nature—
'Cause Nature
Fucks back!

Like their husbands,
These dames got too proud.
They thought they were smarter than Nature,
So what do they get?
Nature drives them all crazy
With lust for *anything* male.
She whips their pussies
To such a man-crazy frenzy
They suddenly needed men
More than ever before . . .

CHUCKLES AT THE MEMORY.

You should have seen them when we arrived!
At first we thought they were attacking
And scrambled into our armor!
Hundreds of them, like starving sea-gulls,
Flocking around us, screeching,
"Men! Men! Men!"
And even while they were running
They were ripping off clothes,
Screaming, "Fuck *me*, O please, please fuck me!
All of you! Fuck me, *please!*"

We couldn't believe it.
It was a teen-age boy's wildest,
Craziest, jerk-off fantasy coming alive!
Some of them lay right down on the beach,
Spreading their legs,
Groaning, squirming, inviting a man
—Any man, they didn't care who—
To get his prick in there and pump!

A few went down on all fours
Hoping a doggy-style invitation
Would get them fucked first—
Ahead of their sisters . . .

Sisters?

There weren't any sisters here.
No friendship, no dignity,
No dreams of a woman's republic.
That was just little girl stuff,
While they waited for men.

Sure, they'd done plenty of talking
But there was just one little problem—
Their cunts and their tits and their wombs
Weren't listening.

You know, for a moment or two
I thought of just sailing away.
Let these dumb bitches die screwing themselves—
And keep their moronic genes
Out of the human pool.

But, what could I do?
My men would never pass up
All that free sex
And, what the hell, at least they'd dilute
Those fools with healthier genes!

So I just told them,
"Up with your thrusting swords, men!
Put 'em out of their misery!"
Not one of them made it a hundred steps up the beach
Before they were down and pumping life into these women . . .

That's when I noticed Medea.
She stood there, staring at all those man-crazy bitches,
But she wasn't laughing.
Not even smiling.
She had this grim look on her face
As if she saw something terrible.
"See how Nature degrades us!" she snarls,
"Uses our bodies—for what?
Your men are getting sore pricks
And these women—what do they get?
Pregnancy, child-birth and slavery to brats!
Men have it so damn easy!
You're Nature's pets!"

"Pets," she says. "Pets."
Yeah, right.
So I told her about the bulls . . .

I was seven or eight
When I saw what they did to bull-calves,
Wham!
Sledge-hammer into the forehead,
Or, for the lucky ones—slice!
Off with their balls to be oxen.

And when I walked home that day
I could see this whole herd of heifers
Drinking milk from their mothers.
Alive.
Happy.
Unmutilated.
And though I was only a kid,
I thought to myself,
'Jason, wake up!
There's a lesson here, boy.

Cows are valuable just as they are.
They only need
Cunts and tits—and they get those at birth.
Cows can just *be*
But bulls?
Bulls have to *do* something special—
Or die . . .'

Deep inside, every man knows that:
Men have to *prove* themselves.
They've got to *do* something special
Or else they don't make it.

Doing.
It's written into our bodies.
Who does all the pumping?
And then?
Millions and millions of sperm
All swimming like crazy,
Racing each other to get to *one* egg—
Her majesty, sitting peacefully on her throne.

Sensitive new-age sperm
Don't make it.

When I said that, she started howling!
"Brood sow—that's all I am to you!
A big fucking brood-sow!"

RE-ENACTING THE CONVERSATION.

"OK, if you want it like that,
You're a big fucking brood sow!
And not just to me—
To Nature!
So what?

You know what I am?
A big dumb machine
For carrying two little balls
The size of a wall-nut!
And what am I good for?
Pumping you up—for 5 seconds or so,
And what am I then?
The pool boy.
'Bring me a drink
And keep strangers out of the yard.'

So welcome to life, little-girl!
Welcome to Nature!
Get used to it, baby,
There's no other show in town.

And while we're at it
Let's straighten out something else:
Without new life, sweetie,
Without any babies, *honey*,
Poetry, art and music
And science and everything else
Don't mean a damn thing!
Without *you*,
And your belly bloated with kids
And your tits full of milk,
Nothing else matters.
Nothing!
Including your pride,
And your dignity or ambition or freedom,
Or your 'glorious womanhood'—
Whatever the hell that means
Without lap full of kids."

TO THE AUDIENCE AGAIN.

And that's what gives women their power!
The dumbest dame in the world
Has more power than any king.
She can make life—and he can't.
She's worth something
Just for that.

The dumbest guy in the world
Isn't worth shit . . .

Except as one the jar-heads
Generals send to die
In a frontal assault . . .

AS IF SUDDENLY THINKING OF SOMETHING.

You know Athena, the virgin goddess of Athens?
She had the snake-haired Medusa
Right on her shield—a warning:
'*This* is what happens to women when they get too far
From their role as life-givers . . . '

And that's what Medea became:
A snake-haired Medusa,
The lowest,
The most *unnatural* thing in the world—
A mother who murders her children.

She slit their throats.

Imagine them screaming,
"No, mommy, no!"
She slaughtered our boys—like pigs!
She drained their blood onto the streets.
She *used* them,

For vengeance on me,
And then tossed them into the trash.

What a chicken-shit bitch!
Don't I sleep?
Stick a knife in my ribs when I'm snoring—
That doesn't take much.
Get a lover to kill me,
Hire a hitter—
But no, Medea, the wanna-be 'leader' of women
Would rather butcher her kids . . .

She trampled,
She pissed and shit on
The most *natural*,
The most *sacred* thing in the world—
A child's trust in its mother.

But, that's Medea
And all her Bitches—
Trampling on Nature,
Twisting, perverting, mutilating
Everything good and natural.

I should have known in Iolcus.

Remember Pelias?
The bastard who killed my father and stole my throne,
Who said I could have it all back
If I brought him the Golden Fleece?
Hoping, of course, I'd get shish-kabobbed by the oxen . . .

Well, my plan was simple and straight—
Like a good man's prick:
Charge into the palace—
"Pelias—The fleece is right here!"

Then slit him open from ass-hole to breakfast
And spill his guts over the floor.
Just like that and it's done.
Who'll object?
It was *my* throne by right:
I'd brought him the fleece like he asked,
He killed my father—and so . . .

SHRUGS.

Medea was horrified,
Stunned by such manly directness.
"If you kill Pelias
His family's on your tail.
But I can fix that
And confuse them so much
They won't even think about you.
Let me handle this—my way."

I was *stupid* enough to listen . . .

Off she goes
To see Pelias's daughters,
None of them smart
But normal, natural children
Who love their father.
She shows them one of the oldest tricks in her book.
She hacks an old ram into pieces
And boils him while babbling some hocus-pocus,
And out pops a frisky young lamb!
"I can do the same for your father," she says,
"He can rule Iolcus forever!"

And the girls go nuts.
They call the old man and Medea shows him the trick
And wets herself laughing!

The old goat wants it so bad,
He's trying to climb in the pot!

Then she hands out the knives
And tells the girls what to do.
The honor is theirs!
And they, of course, balk—
They don't like killing daddy,
But he himself tells them to do it
And next thing you know,
They're sloshing around in his tripes.

And then the grand moment arrives . . .

"Go on, now, make Father young!"
And Medea just laughs in their faces,
"Congratulations!
There's one less man in the world!
Take over the kingdom!
Proclaim yourselves Queens of Iolcus.
I'll use my magical powers
To help you set up a nation
Ruled by, and for women!"

The girls go crazy.
They've murdered their father—
At his command
But who would believe them?
Parent-killers, *that's* what they are.
A crime against Nature,
They're doomed to horrible tortures.
And as for a nation of women,
They don't have a fucking clue what she's talking about.

Meanwhile, there's rioting in the streets,
Mobs shouting "Pelias! Give us Pelias!"

Strangely enough, they believe the girls,
When they said they were tricked,
And give them an easy death.

And, of course, they weren't mad at me.
I was only doing
What law and tradition demanded.
Medea, however,
Well, that was a different story . . .

They were planning her death in detail,
The women leading the way.
"A disgrace to all women!
Rip out her nipples!
Tear out her tongue!
No more magic spells then!
Pass her around to the men!
Roast her alive!"
A cruel and disgusting death
For a cruel and disgusting trick—
Using the natural love of a child
As a tool for revenge.

The horrible irony is
Those yahoos down on the street
Saw the truth before I did—
Medea was really sick shit.
She was *always* using people's natural love
To destroy them—
Her father's love for his son,
The daughters' love for their father,
My love for my sons . . .

They knew the score:
Women love trickery,

That's all part of the game,
But Medea
Was way, *way* out of control.

Of course, at the time,
I wasn't thinking of that.
We were getting the boot from Iolcus.
The King's Council, huffing and puffing with indignation,
Said her trick tainted me.
They'd let the mob burn down Iolcus
And fuck in the ashes
Before I'd ever be king
And as for Medea—
The cheapest old whore in town
Would be their queen before her.
So why don't I just bugger off,
And by the way, wasn't it time
I learned how to be a real man
And keep my woman in line?

I would have—if I'd known how . . .

LAUGHS BITTERLY AT THE IRONY.

Go figure.
Me, Jason, the Argonaut,
Man of a thousand hunts and a hundred battles,
Master of men and horses and ships,
Couldn't control his own woman.

Goddamnit!
Every hill-billy brat
From out in the sticks
Was more of a man than I was.

But what could I do?
Harassing her was no good.
You either left her alone
Or killed her.
Half-measures would only get me
A knife in the ribs some night,
Or a cupful of poisoned wine . . .

The truth is,
I wasn't ready to kill her.
Yet.

Besides, there was no point in talking.
She'd never listen.
She was too bloated
With scorceress pride.

And that's the whole mess in a nutshell
Between Medea and me:
The pride of magic
Against the acceptance of Nature,
Human arrogance
Versus humility,
Sorceress against sailor.

Sailors go places
By *obeying* the wind and the waves,
Not fighting against them.

You accept their power and rules,
And use them to your advantage.
You let them take you
Where *you* want to go.
That
Is the art of sailing . . .

And when a storm comes
Be humble.
Haul down your sails,
Let the sea have its say
And when it's all over,
You just carry on.

But stay proud
And keep your sails hoisted up,
And the winds will rip out your mast
And send you to sleep with the fish.

And don't bother bitching
About the injustice of weather—
Sometimes you have to accept
You're not getting your way,
That's just how it is.

One other thing too:
Don't try to sail over rocks
Just to prove it's your right
To go wherever you want!

   CHUCKLES.

I'm sure you know people who try . . .

Medea was one,
And her Bitches,
Proud of their arrogant magic,
Making rivers run backwards
And drawing the moon from the sky,
Forgetting, the gods made the world
The way it is for a reason.
Maybe we don't understand it,
But that's what we've got to live with . . .

PAUSES TO REFLECT.

After Iolcus, I could have—
I *should* have
Said all these things to Medea,
But, by then we'd landed in Corinth
And, I'll admit,
I had other things on my mind.

I mean, I was starting to wonder
About how loyal she was.
She was always babbling
About the oppression women
And the need for women
To have a state of their own.
Didn't she try stealing Iolcus
Right from under my nose?
That sounded a lot like treason

Meanwhile, she's going ballistic
All of the time.
"Women need power!
No more oppression!
I want to crush male privilege!
I plan to free all women
From slavery to men and Nature!"

I just laughed in her face
Powerless women?
Yeah, right!
What's a marriage proposal?
A guy pleading for his genes
To get into the next generation!
If she refuses, he's toast.
His genes die—forever!

She screeches,
"Who wants that kind of power?
We want political power—like men!"

That's when I let her have it,
Right in the kisser.
"Sweetie, *that* kind of power
Belongs *first of all*,
To those who take all the risks,
And do all the dirty work—
Men!

And you want to know why?

Because like it or not,
Mother Nature can be a real bitch!
She kicks lots of ass
—I listed them all in detail—
Fire, drought, flood, earthquake,
Freezing winters, epidemics,
Famine, insects, ice-storms, hurricanes,
Hail, tornadoes, crop diseases,
Tidal waves and early winters,
Late springs, changing ocean currents,
And, just for more fun,
Ice-ages every ten thousand years or so . . ."

At this point she's screaming and holding her ears,
And I haven't even started
On all the man-made disasters,
Or human predators coming in all sorts of gangs.

"So it's plain as can be,
As long as the *good times* last,
Women can *play* at having political power—
But when push comes to shove

And the shit's on the fan,
When Mother Nature
Has kicked your ass through the wall,
It's a *man's* world, baby,
And always will be.
'Cause really tough times
Mean pushing and pulling,
And hunting and killing
And all the stuff guys do best.
So,
For the good of *all,*
We're in charge."

"So we're just servants, are we?
Brood sows,
Earning our bed and board
By getting raped?"

PAUSES, AGITATED, THEN PULLS HIMSELF TOGETHER.

Rape was her big obsession.
She'd never been raped,
But, you know, there are women
Who, for some reason,
Love to pretend they have.
It makes them feel so important
And gives them some kind of sick thrill.
It makes me wonder if deep down inside
They wouldn't mind a small taste . . .

Anyway, one day I blew.
"Listen, you stupid bitch,
I've got news for you—
Rape
Believe or not,
Is *not* the worst thing that happens to people.

Yes, *people*, you ignorant snot,
Men get raped too!
Remember galleys and prisons.
The hard, bitter truth is
Rape
Is survivable!
Most women
—*And* men—
Live through it!
It may not be fun
But it beats the hell out of dying!

You know what you can't survive?
A set of horns in your guts,
Or a spear in your crotch!

And you know how men get those things?
Hunting—or fighting—for women and kids.

So face it, a woman is born
With her life-insurance
Between her legs!
That's the source
Of her *natural*
Female
Privilege!
That's what keeps them from risky jobs
And safe in the office . . ."

I yelled it right in her face:
"Your cunt is your ticket to safety!
Your tits are your passport
To extra water and food,
You're pregnant, you're nursing, you're bleeding,
And so you get shelter and warmth,
And when the boat's sinking

Guess who goes to the life-boats
Ahead of the men and the boys?
Your cunt, honey-bunch,
Gets you promotions.
A good-looking peasant girl
Can screw her way to the top—
How many guys can do that?

And when nations collapse
Women get taken as slaves,
They're valuable,
They can make life—
The men and the boys
Get

HE GESTURES THROAT SLITTING.

Guys are the ones who carry
Death-warrants in their crotches!
That's how it is, baby,
That's
How it *really* is!"

These days I call women like her
'Titanic feminists',
You know the kind.
Equality—
'Til the iceberg hits.
Then they turn into women
And want first place in the life-boats

She didn't hear a damn thing,
She just screeches—
God, don't she and her Bitches
Always screech?
"So we like rape, do we?

THE GENDER WARS TRILOGY 103

We're all just waiting to get it
From any guy with a hard-on?"

Women—
What have they got against logic?
That's not what I said.
I said being raped and alive
Is better than dying . . .
Who's going to argue with that?

Anyway, around this time,
Things heated up in Corinth.
You see, I met Creon, the king,
And Glauce, his daughter.
Twenty years old,
A real beauty, but more important,
One of those rare
Women who could face facts . . .

"Men are stirring spoons,
Women are pots.
For better or worse,
Men stir things up
And women turn all this stirring
Into good soup.
No spoon,
No pot,
Means
No soup!"

What a relief—
Common sense in a girl!
But don't kid yourself—
She was no ditz.

"Men are like dogs—
Trainable, but
You've got to work with what's there!"
Then she scratched the ears
Of this wolf-hound that flopped at her feet,
And smiled at me as she said,
"Do want me to scratch your ears too?"

Had I been insulted—or flattered?
You know, after three thousand years
I still can't tell which.
All I know is, I loved it . . .

She helped me understand women.

"Of course we take everything personally.
Being a mother
Is *all* about being personal.
Just like being a wife.
Women make everything
Into a personal issue.
Only a stupid man
Ever forgets that . . ."

Objective, pure logic, she said,
Was really a man-thing,
Simple and straight, like a prick.
You were in or out,
You got off or you didn't,
You won or you lost,
Nothing half-way
And no shading.
One way or the other—
But women?
Nothing was quite that simple for them.

"Women are messier.
We've got too much to juggle
To be as straight-forward as you.
That's why we've got to be
What men call 'tricky'—
To juggle all the complexity in our lives."

And then she just laughed,
A beautiful, natural laughter.
I was enchanted the moment I heard it.
I envied her dog.
Would you believe it?
—I, Jason—
The world famous Argonaut
Envied the mutt at her feet.

Glauce knew from the start
Medea was just a boss cow
Gone nuts.

You know what a boss cow is?
When there's no bull
One cow decides she's the boss
And bullies the others.
She even mounts them . . .

That was Medea, all right.

They'd met:
Medea, the hard-ball player,
And Glauce,
The 'soft power' expert.
Rock
Against water.
Slash
Against smile.

Glauce naived Medea to death.
When Medea comes storming in
About a women's republic
And feminine sisterhood,
Glauce just hauled down her sail
And acts like a ditzy dame.

JASON MIMICS GLAUCE PLAYING WITH MEDEA.

"Oh my—no men?
But my little pot needs a spoon!
A week without fucking
And I'm a real bitch!
You've *got* to admit,
There's something addictive in sperm!"

LAUGHS.

Medea's just stunned!
She doesn't know what to say,
So she blabbers about keeping some men
—But they'd better be good—
And Glauce goes, "Oh!
You want to beat out their spirits?
But surely, Medea, you know,
If men can't stand up by day
They can't stand up at night!
That's just how they are!"

That was enough for Medea.
Rolling her eyes and muttering under her breath
She stomps out of the palace.
Glauce and all her ladies were smirking.
They thought it was funny.

That was a bad mistake.

We
—And I more than anyone else—
Should have known better
Than ever to laugh at Medea.
We were so happy, we overlooked
Her incredible talent
For reaching extremes
And going too far . . .

As a wedding gift
She gave Glauce a cloak,
Beautiful beyond words.
She brought it into the palace,
Saying it was a token
Of reconcilement and friendship
And sisterhood among women,
And bowed and scraped her way out . . .

JASON RE-ENACTS THE WHOLE EVENT.

"Glauce—no!
Don't put it on!"

Too late!
A long, piercing scream,
Flames shoot out of her crotch,
Licking her nipples, her breasts,
Swelling and bloating and—
God!
Her breasts explode!
Blood raining down!
Burning blood!
Her legs

—Her back—
Split open!
Her spine
Snaps—
Like a stick!
She's down!
Twisting and struggling,
Screaming.
"—Creon, don't touch her!—
You'll burn!"
Her face splits open!
Blood's spurting out!
She screams out a mouthful of fire!
Smoke's pouring out of her belly—
Her belly bursts open!
She rolls to me,
Hand up in prayer
I jump back—
If I touch her, I'll burn—
Oh God.
God!
GOD—
Where the fuck are you?

PAUSES, RECOLLECTING HIMSELF FOR THE AUDIENCE.

That
Was the hardest fight of my life.
I had to beat up my heart
To a bloody pulp
So I wouldn't jump to her rescue.

I had a duty to live.
I had sons to look after . . .

THE GENDER WARS TRILOGY   109

Besides, I wanted to catch
And torture Medea—
Skin her slowly—alive!
I'd start by peeling her face,
Her eyebrows and cheeks and lips,
Then I'd work my way down
Her neck, her nipples and breasts,
By God, I'd pickle her
One little piece at a time . . .

You think I'm a vicious, sadistic bastard, don't you?
Don't you?
You know what she did while Glauce was burning alive?

She killed our sons . . .

One had to watch
As she slit the other one's throat!
Watch, as his brother
Cringes in terror,
"Oh Mommy, good Mommy, no!"
Then the hiss
Of cut flesh and muscle splitting apart,
Blood spurts from his veins.
He gurgles,
Blood's frothing out of his mouth,
In a thick red foam,
And he's heaving and gasping for breath
As he drowns in his blood.
She drags him, drops him
Head down on the steps
So his blood drains onto the street.
Then she goes for his brother,
She mocks them for not fighting back!
She tells him I'll be ashamed,
I'll hate them for crying . . .

And then, with her filthy magic
She summons her witch's chariot,
Drawn by the dragons of time
Past, present and future,
And drives away into the sky.
Laughing,
Laughing like long rolls of thunder,
And smiling like lightning . . .

She
—Medea, the mother—
The woman who wants to lead women,
Stood on the soft, blood-less flesh
Of her sons.

They were softer than metal, she said,
And warmer than brass . . .

She isn't fit to stand
On a pile of pig-shit!

This is the woman they weep for—
Euripedes, Ovid and Jeffers
And all those fools
Who never once faced her evil.

And now, she's here, in your age,
Trying to spread her disease.

And it's working.
She grows like a plague among you,
Perverting your laws,
Infecting your children,

Polluting your minds and your hearts,
Sowing division and conflict!
And never before has she found
Such a harvest of fools!

Women
—And men—
Ready, willing, eager,
Running to join her cult
Of hatred for Nature and men.

And why not?
It feels good,
Hate makes you feel alive and strong,
It gives you a sense of purpose and value,
It pulls you together.
It doesn't have to make sense,
It can be stupid as shit—
Just look at Medea.
If a quarter of what she says about women is true,
If women have been bamboozled
And bullied for thousands of years,
What does it prove except women
Are weak—*and* stupid enough
To knuckle under so long?

Hatred has made her so stupid
She can't understand
Her views *degrade* women
More than anything ever said
By dumb-ass men.

She and her arrogant Bitches
Actually think they're the first
Women with guts and brains,
The first to discover the truth
About Nature and men!

As if our fore-mothers
Were helpless cows
Too stupid to kill a man
In his sleep.

But wait!
It gets crazier still!
She and her Bitches believe
Being a woman's
Got *nothing* to do with a cunt
Or tits,
Let alone having kids—

PAUSES TO LET THIS SINK IN.

Take all these things away
And what do you get?
Not even a eunuch!
Only some sexless thing,
Some brain concoction
That doesn't exist in Nature.
Next they'll say being a man
Has nothing to do with balls!

And isn't that just like Medea?
Knife-work!
Surgery.
Amputation.
I remember how she used to praise
The Amazons—you know,
The women who cut off a tit
So they could be more like a man?

Nowadays lots of 'progressive' women
Are cutting off tits
For the same reason.
Except now they give it
A fancier name
—'De-constructing' gender!—
But it boils down to cutting off tits,
And balls!
That's where Medea wants to go next
With her knife!

You'd think every man in the world
Would resist—but oh no,
We've got these guys
—Sensitive new age guys—
Standing in line,
Holding out balls and pricks
All ready to get the bobbit!
They *want* to get sliced!
'Cause they're all convinced
Testosterone's evil.
They call themselves the '*new men*',
But *I* call them *Wee Willy Wet Legs*—
Little boys, frightened of women
And scared of being real men!

There've always been guys like that.
In my day they were the priests of Cybele—
She was a goddess
Whose men had to cut off their balls
And hang them in 'sacred' pines,
Sort of like Christmas tree decorations . . .

SINGS MOCKINGLY.

'On the first day of Christmas, my true love gave to me,
His testicles in a pine tree!'

She calls this trick
The 'hydrogen bomb of the gender wars'—
Turning billions of men
Into sensitive new age guys
With small, shrunken balls
Or no balls at all
And small, shrunken heads,
All eager to be like the girls.
Well,
It's going to be a big fizzle . . .

She doesn't have a clue
How tricky Nature can be—
Or men . . .

The truth is,
A *lot* of those Wee Willy Wet Legs
Are secretly working for me!
They're Nature's—and *my*—fifth column
Deep inside enemy lines!

She and her Bitches
—Like all other women—
Have fallen for fancy words!
Sure, those sensitive new age guys
Talk the right talk
And make the right noises in public.
Sure, they act sorry
For having testosterone
But you want to know why?

They've discovered *this*
Is the new way to get
Their hands up a skirt!
To them it's just guy talk
To get to the holy of holies!
There's nothing a man won't say
To get there.
And then what?
Babies!
Unleashing those motherhood instincts
In millions of bitter bitches,
Letting them find a woman's natural pleasures
In goo-eyes, smilies and burpies
And baby's first little steps!

And when those bitches taste that,
Before you know it, they're off
On the mommy-track,
Off to the world of half-time careers
So they can be moms—at home,
Loving, soothing, *nurturing.*
Back to a woman's main job!

While men keep right on advancing
Straight to the top . . .

Medea and all her Bitches
Are standing out there in public
Ready to fight,
But who really cares?
They're waiting on the wrong battle-field!
That's not where the real action is!
The real action happens wherever

Pants and panties come down,
Bedrooms, back-seats, on beaches, in bushes,
Wherever the two-backed beast
Rocks—to start cradles rocking.
And *nothing* will ever stop that!

SITS DOWN, AT EASE; A SELF-CONTENTED SIGH.

Poor Medea.
Beating her is so easy.
I don't have to do a thing
Except sit here—and wait
For Nature to do all the work!

I guess in a way,
I'm Russian:
I let the invaders advance
To their own destruction.
I don't kill them—
I help them die.
Let Nature destroy them.
It doesn't matter to me
How my enemies lose
As long as they do . . .
Freezing winters or mud—
Or the sizzle of sex
And the cry for life in the womb—

Winning is all that matters . . .

Already I've seen
A few of her Bitches deserting,
Back to Nature,
To me . . .

HE SALUTES WITH A DRINK.

I love the smell of semen in the morning—
It smells like—victory!

LAUGHS.

Medea forgot,
I'm a hunter, a killer, a sailor,
A Taoist who knows how to wait
And let a storm pass,
And how to sit still
In a blind—or an ambush.
I know the secret
Of doing nothing
At the right time
So my enemies get lots of room
To destroy themselves.

And the Bitches who stay with Medea?
The truth is,
I *want* them to stay
Right where they are—
No kids,
And if they're knocked up,
I hope they abort.

Either way,
They clean up the gene-pool.

And if they raise kids,
I hope they poison them all with their lies.
Those brats will be so damn bitter,
So sick and twisted inside
Kids from people like Glauce and me
Will find them easy to rule!

And the Wee Willy Wet Legs?
—I mean those who aren't secretly working for me—
Hurry! Don't wait!
Cut off your balls!
Take your trash out of the gene pool!
It'll be great
Not seeing your face in the future!

LIFTS A GLASS IN A MOCK TOAST.

So party it up, Medea.
I'm cheering each one of your Bitches
And every kid you don't have!
I salute every guy who cuts off his balls,
I salute every homosexual pounding another ass
Every lesbian licking a cunt—
The more, the better!
Really, I hope you have fun
While removing yourselves from the future
'Cause fun's all you'll ever have!
And when the fun's over,
It's over—
The Big O doesn't last forever!

But Nature does.
And in the long run
Nature
Always wins . . .

So don't worry, you natural guys and girls,
Don't worry about Medea and all her Bitches
And Wee Willy Wet Legs parading around without balls!
Ride out the storm!
Rest in your blind!
Keep cover in ambush!

They're already weakening,
They've run out of steam,
They're fighting amongst themselves.
Soon we'll counter-attack,
And sweep these lunatics right off the boards
And into the trash!

Nature—and people like us—
Are headed for victory . . .

Trust me—I'm Jason, the Argonaut.
Though I'm speaking to you through this actor,
My spirit's alive as ever
And sharp as my favorite sword.
Don't worry—we'll win.
I'm a sailor and hunter and warrior,
I'm an old hand at this game
And I know how it's played . . .

*HE POURS HIMSELF ANOTHER DRINK AND GIVES HIS RIFLE
ANOTHER QUICK BUFF. THEN HE PICKS UP A BOOK AND
LEANS BACK AND STARTS TO READ.*

LIGHTS FADE

A MARRIAGE MADE IN HELL

Note

This wedding is like a knife-fight: the combatants circle each other, seeking the fatal opening, the victorious lunge. The witnesses circle too, watching, hoping, trying to help one person or another.

CHARACTERS

Jason
Medea
Ian
Aetes
Glauce
Hecabe
Cadmus
Pentheus

THE THEATRE AND THE STAGE IS DECORATED FOR A WEDDING. AS MEMBERS OF THE AUDIENCE ENTER, EACH PERSON IS HANDED A 'WEDDING PROGRAM'. THEY PASS THROUGH AN ARCHWAY. SOLEMN AND ROMANTIC WEDDING MUSIC IS PLAYED OVER THE PA SYSTEM.

THE ALTAR IS DECORATED WITH THE DOUBLE AXE OF CRETE. THERE IS A PODIUM, COVERED WITH WHITE CLOTH.

MEDEA ENTERS THROUGH THE SAME DOORS AS THE AUDIENCE. AS SHE ENTERS, IAN QUICKLY PUTS A BRIDAL CROWN AND VEIL ON HER HEAD.

MEDEA
Screeching as she throws it off.

What the fuck's going on?
What is all this shit?
A wedding—
A goddamn wedding!

*AT THAT MOMENT JASON ENTERS FROM THE SAME
DOORS.*

JASON
Sarcastic

Aw, isn't that sweet!
A wedding!
Well, screw you Kluge,
Not with this boy you don't . . .

*HE TURNS OUT THE DOOR BUT IS CAUGHT UP BY
IAN WHO TAKES HIM DECISIVELY BY THE ARM AND
FORCEFULLY 'ESCORTS' HIM BACK INTO THE
THEATRE.*

IAN
In a policeman's 'come along' tone of voice.

Come on now,
Nobody's going to hurt you . . .

*HE MARCHES JASON DOWN THE AISLE TOWARDS
MEDEA WHO IS STILL STANDING IN SHOCK AND
MUTTERING TO HERSELF WHILE THE OTHER ACTION
GOES ON: "I CAN'T BELIEVE THIS . . . THIS IS FUCKING
OUTRAGEOUS . . . THAT BASTARD . . . ETC."*

JASON
Angry and still thrashing somewhat

Get your paws off me or I'll kill you!
Nobody man-handles Jason!

IAN

I do—
Because I'm the author.
Kill me and this play
—*And* this performance—
Wouldn't exist,
And [*name of actor*] wouldn't be here
To lend you his body
So your spirit could speak to us.

TO MEDEA

You can relax, my dear.
Before you know it,
He'll be your husband at last.

MEDEA
Disgusted

Husband my ass!
He never *was* my husband—
And *never* will be!

JASON

Exactly.

IAN

We'll see.

MEDEA

Like hell!
I left him three thousand years ago.
What do I want with him now?
I'm not a dog,
I don't go back to my puke!

JASON

I couldn't agree with you more.

MEDEA

Why don't you shut up?

JASON

Because that would make you happy.

*HE TURNS TO IAN. HE IS MORE COMPOSED,
THOUGH STILL TESTY.*

You want to tell me what's happening?
You invite me to discuss my future in your plays
And then you do this—
A wedding!
A goddamn wedding . . .

IN A SOMEWHAT THREATENING TONE OF VOICE

This better be good . . .

MEDEA

Damn rights!
'Cause I'm a pretty pissed bitch!

JASON
Dryly

What else is new?
Nothing's changed in 3000 years—
Except now you run the Women's Studies Department!

IAN

This *is* your future in my plays:
I want you two married.

JASON
Feigning stupidity; points to the appropriate people as he speaks.

Now, let's see if I got this right:
You
Want her and me.
Married.

IAN

Bingo.

MEDEA
To Ian

What the hell gives you the right—

JASON
To Medea

Nobody gives men rights.
They take them.
That's how it is with Nature

MEDEA

Both of you—
Just damn pushy men!

JASON

You still don't get it—
Pushing
Is what men do!
It's the essence of maleness!
Push the other guys out of the way.
Push in the penis
And push in the sperm
That pushes its way to the target!

MEDEA

Do you ever think about anything but your prick?

JASON
Mock surprise

Medea!
You're getting mellow!
In the old days you would have said,
'Do you ever think
With anything but your prick?'
But I guess you've learned
My brain
Thinks *for* my crotch

Just like *real* women
—Not wanna-be men
Like you and your feminazis—
Think *for* their cunts.
They look for quality guys
With quality sperm
So they don't birth trash.
That's
Mother Nature's way.

MEDEA

Since you know her so well
Tell the old bag
She's getting a boot in the ass
From a new gang of women
Who plan to be more
Than peg-boards for men.

JASON

My God!
So it's true!
Female ghosts
Still suffer from PMS!

IAN
Ignoring them

Look guys,
You've had your own plays to say this.
But this isn't just your play,
It's *ours*—
And above all, *mine*.

MEDEA

I tell you right now
It's not happening.

IAN
Disingenuously

What's not happening?

JASON

This wedding shit.

MEDEA
Outraged

You're crazy!
What makes you think we'd ever get married?

IAN

Because you're made for each other!

BOTH JASON AND MEDEA LOOK AT HIM WITH INCOMPREHENSION.

Come on, you've got to admit
Yours
Is a marriage made in hell!

MEDEA

And that's why . . .

IAN

Who cares where it's made?
At least it's made *somewhere*.
Not like most marriages
That are made nowhere,
And therefore have nowhere to grow.

JASON

Last I heard marriage needs love.

IAN

But of course!
And who's more in love than you?

JASON

We haven't screwed in 3000 years!

IAN

Some couples make love in bed,
And others make love in the ring . . .

In fact, you've been making love
In public for 3000 years!
It takes tons of love
To keep a fight going that long!

MEDEA
Outraged

You call that 'making love'?

IAN

Absolutely!
You're so deeply in love,
You need each other so much,
You can't stay away from each other.

MOCK PLEADING TO MEDEA

Aw, face it, Medea,
You want a sparring partner,
Not some sweet lover boy
Bringing you flowers
And whispering nothings into your ear.
You want a guy
Who brings a bouquet of knives,
And challenges you to a slash-dance.
Weasel girl, that's what you are.
For getting it on
You need to bite and be bitten.
You like to test your guys first.
You need a guy with an edge
Like your own—
Him

POINTS TO JASON AND THEN SAYS TO MEDEA

You're his real woman,
Looking for quality sperm . . .

MEDEA

You're a sick son-of-a-bitch.

IAN
Blasé

Probably.
But am I right?

JASON
Threateningly

Don't think I'm stupid, Kluge,
I smell the trap.
You're trying to make us think
Our fight's just an act,
Some incredibly fancy
3000 year mating dance.
Well, let me tell you,
I 'ain't' no stork.

IAN
Laughing

Ah, so you know I'm right!

MEDEA
Outraged

I don't give a fuck if you're right.
If you think I'm giving up
At my moment of victory,
You're crazy!

JASON
Incredulous

Your moment of what?

MEDEA

You heard me.

JASON

I did—
I was just giving you a chance
To correct your mistake.

MEDEA

And what mistake's that?

JASON

The victory bit.

MEDEA
Shaking her head.

You still don't get it.
You still haven't figured out
Troy the Testosterone's dead.
The patriarchy's on fire!
Burning!
It's blowing away in the wind
Like ashes . . .

JASON
Contemptuously

Are you saying that women have won?

MEDEA
Laughs and then exultantly

Won?
Oh no, not won!

*LOOKING AROUND; THIS SPEECH IS GIVEN TO THE
AUDIENCE AS MUCH AS TO JASON.*

Triumphed!
Women have *triumphed!*
Look around you—everywhere
Men want to be like women,
Sensitive new age guys,
No balls, and sickened with guilt
About their testosterone!
Ashamed of their fathers!
Ashamed of their maleness
And its constant jiggery-pokery
At every hole and crack
No matter where or in what!

Yes! We've won.
It took us a million years
But at last
We have the whip.
And now, by the Goddess,
We'll use it!

JASON
Blandly

And?

MEDEA

That's not enough?
But wait!

TAKES ON A 'BRACING HERSELF' STANCE

OK . . . OK, I'm ready now.
Hit me with some of your manly 'wisdom'.

JASON

Nothing so grand.
Just a plain, simple fact.
Victory isn't enough.
You can win the war
And lose it all in the peace.
It's what you do with the victory—
That's what matters!

WITH AN AMUSED CURIOSITY

And what will you do
With *your* victory?

MEDEA
Laughs; she is working herself into a lather of triumphalism

Do with it? Ha!
Where do I start?
We'll flog you to ribbons—
Flog 'til our whips wear out
And our arms collapse!
Then we'll humiliate you—
Kick you all down, degrade you

Like you've been degrading us
With sex and childbirth
And motherhood slavery.
Millions of years
You enslaved us,
Kept us down on our backs
Shitting *your* brats into this world
And while we're screaming,
You—you pricks—
What are *you* doing?
Fucking some other dumb cunt
All eager to get the same.
But now, it's different.
Women are waking up!
We've got you on your knees
And damn it! You'll stay there
'Til every women
Has pissed herself laughing!

JASON
Enthusiastically

Right on!
Flog'em to bits.
Weed out the weak!
Whack all the Wee Willy Wet-Legs!
Take out those whimpering, mewling men
Those sensitive new age guys
So willing to shame themselves
And piss on their father's grave.
Castrate'em *all*
Before they pollute the planet
With their wimp-genes.
Damn it, I'll even help you!

MEDEA
Coldly

We don't need your help.

JASON
Eagerly

Of course you don't *need* my help.
But like it or not,
I'm on your side!
Like you,
I'm eager to do my bit
To improve *man*-kind.

MEDEA
Laughs and then contemptuously

That's a loser's trick, Jason:
Find the parade
And put yourself at the front.

But not this time, boy.
This time
Women will march on their own!
We've got our pride!

JASON
'Shocked'

But Medea,
War's not about pride—
It's about winning!
Allies
Don't have to be friends.

MEDEA

We'll do things our way,
Not yours.

JASON

You mean like Lemnos?

MEDEA
Contemptuously

You'd like that, wouldn't you?
We get rid of men
And in few years
There's a world of man-crazy women
Who want to do nothing but fuck.

Well, I'm not that stupid, Jason.
I learned from Lemnos.
I know that won't work.
Most women aren't ready
For life without men.
Someday—maybe,
But not for a while.
So, we'll have men
In my feminist new world order
But men on *our* terms,
Not yours.

SARCASTICALLY SWEET.

If we can't clip you between the legs
We'll clip you between the ears.

We'll have you
Just like a horse,
Beautiful, useful, and
—For those who still enjoy rape—
Maybe even some fun.
But, let me tell you
We'll be in control.
You'll be something *we* train
With bridles and snaffle-bars, halters and—

JASON

Whips.

MEDEA
Vehemently

And whips, if that's what it takes!
And you want to know something?

LAUGHING

Most men won't mind
As long as they get some!
Grab a guy by the balls
And his brains will follow.

JASON
'Amazed'

By God, you're starting to understand us
And our endless perversity!
You know, before long
Men will be *wanting* the whip

To help get us off!
And your girls will be wearing
Cute little whipping skirts
To add to the fun.

CHUCKLES

And we all know where *that* leads . . .

IAN STEPS IN.

IAN
Beaming

Now look at you two—
Such *passion*,
Such *wit*—
You're perfectly *made* for each other.
You'll have a blast
For another 3000 years!
So let's not waste time
And get started.

*COMPOSES HIMSELF TO LOOK SERIOUS, THEN
TURNS TO THE AUDIENCE.*

Dearly beloved,
By the power invested in me as a playwright
And thus, second only to God,
Who made his own heaven and earth
As I did mine,
Let us begin these nuptials
Of history's most amorous couple,
Medea and Jason.

Is there anyone here
Who would like the honor

Of witnessing these vows
On behalf of the groom?

AETES
Standing up in the audience

I will.

IAN

And you are?

AETES

Aetes, Medea's father.
Obviously, she would not consent to be given away,
So, I will stand for her husband-to-be instead.

IAN

Your reasons?

AETES

Revenge.

IAN

Revenge?
At a wedding?

AETES
Moving out of the audience.

Sweet, blessed, *holy* vengeance.
She murdered my son,
She stole the wealth of my kingdom.

She turned me and my queen into fools.
All for this man.
Now I want her to get what she wanted.

JASON

Why?

AETES

There's no other way
For her to atone for her crimes
Than by marrying you.

IAN
To audience

Do you think we can accept a witness
With motives like these?

AETES
To audience

My motives are all for her best.
By marrying him
She can make up for her crimes.
Atonement will bring forgiveness—
And she has much to forgive:
Killing her ten year old brother
To escape from my ships.
She cut his flesh into pieces
And threw them into the sea.
She knew I would stop
To retrieve the remains of my son.
She committed treason against her nation,
Stealing the Golden Fleece, our national treasure,
And betrayed her moon-priestess vows,

And humiliated her parents.
Without forgiveness,
How could she ever find peace?

JASON
Challenging

So I'm her punishment?

AETES

Punishment
Is also a medicine.
You are her way to peace.
If she can have that
Perhaps our losses
Will have some meaning.

JASON

And if I refuse?

AETES
Vehemently

You cannot.
She committed her crimes,
But *you* led her to them.
You owe her this much—
And us.

JASON

I owe you nothing, old man,
Except a kick in the ass!

AETES

It's time you were an old man
And stopped being a boy—*boy*!

JASON
Flippantly

Ever notice how losers
Like taking the moral high ground?

AETES

Do you think you're one of the gods
And can't lose?

JASON

I haven't lost yet.

AETES
Shocked and amazed

'I haven't lost yet'

TO AUDIENCE.

Do you hear what a child this is?
His two sons were murdered
And yet he brags,
'I haven't lost yet'.

TO JASON.

You had two sons,
But they never lived in your heart.
They were dead there

THE GENDER WARS TRILOGY 143

Before she murdered their bodies!
She only finished up
What you started.

You never had any children,
All you ever had was spasms
Inside a woman.
Your flesh
Spawned more flesh,
But you've never been a father
Or you wouldn't say
'I haven't lost yet'.
Not with two children dead . . .

HE ADVANCES ALMOST THREATENINGLY ON JASON.

Now let me give you some news, *boy.*
My ships could have taken the Argo that day
When you escaped with the fleece,
But I was a father
—Something you don't understand—
And I had to choose the fleece
Or the flesh of a son
Betrayed and butchered
By my own daughter.
Do you know
What it's like to feel the two halves of your heart
Ripping each other apart?
Of course not—
But *that's* why you got away!
Not because you were better,
But because I
Was a human being,
A man,
A father.
What father could think of the Golden Fleece that day?

JASON

I loved my sons
As much as anyone could.

AETES

Then you've been a loser, boy—
Big time.
You've lost so big
No victories on this earth
Could even start making it right.
But you're spouting nothing but cock-talk.
That tells me
You don't have a clue what you've lost.

CHALLENGING JASON.

Look around you, boy,
Look at these people.
Do you see your sons?
Do you see them?
No!
They're not here.
The only ones here
Are those who lived in your heart,
And your sons aren't out there.

GESTURES TO THE AUDIENCE

MEDEA

I saw them!

AETES
Quietly

No, Medea, you didn't.
If they were here
They would call you 'Mother'
And you'd be ashamed and embarrassed.
You'd want to raise them like girls
Instead of loving them as they are.
Didn't you say once
They raped you from inside out?
No mother says that.
You were just flesh
That dropped two little sacks of flesh
Into this world,
But a woman, a mother?
Never . . .

SHAKES HIS HEAD.

The truth is
You'll never see them again.
They are at rest in the arms
Of the Great Mother Goddess,
She, of a thousand sweet faces,
She, of a thousand sweet names,
Who holds all unwanted children in her embrace.
You'll never see them again
Not even in dreams . . .
And they—thank God—won't see you
And remain at peace.
If you've discovered love for them now
Show it by staying away.

MEDEA MAINTAINS A SOBER SILENCE AND LOOKS AWAY.

But enough,
Let's finish this wedding . . .

JASON
Bitterly

Nobody made you come here,
Nobody made you volunteer as a witness
So leave.
With my blessings.

AETES

Your blessings?
Then I'll be sure not to go.
When you give blessings
Somebody always
Gets tripped into hell.

JASON

Have it your way,
'Cause on way or another,
I'm leaving.

AETES

Again?

JASON

Yes, again.

AETES

Isn't that what you always do
When the going gets rough?

JASON
Blandly

'He who fights and runs away
Lives to fight another day.'

AETES

That's you to the core:
Hit and run fighter,
Hit and run fucker.
But hit and run never ruled a pig-pen
Much less a kingdom.
And isn't that what you wanted?
To rule a kingdom?

JASON

When I find it.

AETES
Laughs

You haven't found it
In 3,000 years.
Doesn't that tell you something?

JASON SAYS NOTHING.

You know what it says?

You aren't fit to rule.
You aren't fit to be king.
You know why?
Because you're a *boy*,
And you think like a boy,
And you act like a boy.
You know what a boy is at heart?
A pirate!
A free-loader, a raider,
A here-today gone-tomorrow free-fucker
Who thinks of himself number one.
Oh yes, he wins,
But he only wins for himself
And he always skips out
'Cause hanging around's not his style.

PAUSES, PULLING HIMSELF TOGETHER AND THEN
CONTINUES.

But a king—
A real king and not some pirate
Just wearing a crown,
A king, in case you've never noticed
—*Boy*—
Is someone who sticks around
Especially when things get rough.
His people, his city
—Not him—
Are his first
And second
And third concerns,
And when even one widow weeps
A real king can't sleep for worry
That somehow he missed his duty.

Pelias who stole your throne

Was a *real* king.
He murdered your father
But ruled so well
His people
—Who should have been *your* people—
Would rather burn down the city than have you as king.
Why is that, boy?
When they looked at you,
What was so obvious—
Even to red-necks and dumb hoi-poloi,
That made them say, '*Never!*'

JASON SAYS NOTHING.

I know what they saw,
And I'll tell you.
They saw a raw boy,
A pirate,
Tough and brave
And full of shrewd tricks
To get what he wanted.
Smart as a whip,
But boy-smart,
Not man-smart,
Not king-smart . . .

You know the difference?
Boy smart is right as far as it goes—
It just doesn't go very far.

You talk lots about nature and being natural,
And the power of genes,
How women will leave Medea
And go back to their natural selves.
You talk about being a killer and hunter,
And all of it's true.

Every last word.
You'll win.

But a killer and hunter is *all* that you are.
You'll win—but you'll never rule
Because *after* the hunt
You've got to share out the meat
And eat with your people.
You've got to settle their quarrels
And put on a show.
You've got to balance all kinds of accounts—
A lot of the time at your own expense.
Because you're the king
You can't always win
Like a boy.
Sometimes a king
Has to know when to lose for his people . . .

STARES AT JASON INTENSELY.

They didn't see that in you.
And so they picked an excuse,
Medea's trick on Pelias's daughters,
To boot your ass out the door!

And you say you've never lost?

You mean you're too much of a boy,
Too much of cock-proud pirate
To see how badly you've lost.
3,000 years
And what have you got to show for it?
Not even fame—
Just *notoriety* as a clever-ass pirate . . .

*LAUGHS DISDAINFULLY LOUD AND LONG AS THE
OTHERS LOOK ON IN SHOCKED SILENCE.*

IAN
Rubbing his hands somewhat nervously, trying to overcome the tension.

Well then, where were we?
I think Aetes will serve as a witness,

THERE IS A COMMOTION FROM THE AUDIENCE.

GLAUCE
Standing up

I'll give Jason away.

MEDEA, JASON

Glauce?

GLAUCE
Freshly, almost flippant

In the flesh, so to speak,
Thanks to *[actress name]*

JASON
Shocked, dismayed

But . . . you were marrying me!

MEDEA
Snarling

What are doing here, bitch?

GLAUCE
Breezily

Giving you a husband.
It's the least I can do
For burning me live at my wedding . . .

TO JASON.

I *was* marrying you—
But not any more . . .

MEDEA

I don't want him,
Especially from you.

GLAUCE

Oh no, Medea, you *must!*
It's *your* turn to burn,
So he's yours,
All yours,
Forever.

MEDEA
Snarling

Like hell!
I don't like hand-me-downs.

GLAUCE

This is a hand-me-back.

JASON
Heart-broken

Glauce!
What are you doing?
Don't you love me?

GLAUCE
Sincerely

I love you with all my heart!

JASON

Then how can you—

GLAUCE

My loving *you* has got nothing to do with it, Jason.
The truth is, you don't belong with me—
You belong with her.

JASON
Protesting vehemently

But I love you!

GLAUCE
Patiently, as with a child.

Jason, you loved me because I wasn't Medea,
Not because I was me.

JASON

And?

GLAUCE

That's not enough to build on.
Not being Medea
Is not who I am.
I'm me!

JASON

I don't understand . . .

MEDEA

Praise the Goddess!

TO AUDIENCE.

Did you hear that?
Jason,
The great, cunning Jason
Just said,
'I don't understand'—
To a woman!

TO GLAUCE.

O baby, he's yours for sure.
This is your wedding,
And this time,
No presents from me . . .

GLAUCE
Ignoring Medea; going towards Jason

Listen.
I'll try to explain . . .
Loving me for not being Medea
Is not the same as *loving me*
For what I am.
It means Medea will always be with us
'Cause you didn't love me
You loved the difference between us . . .

Her shadow will always be there,
When we make love, or when I have children
Or when we're just walking together.
And I'm too much of a woman
To share you with somebody else,
Even a ghost.

JASON

Ignore her!
I do!

GLAUCE

I can't—and you don't.
You've been obsessed with her
For 3,000 years!

I'm a woman, Jason,
I'm jealous,
I want all of you
Or I want nothing.
Do you understand?

JASON

Yes, but I can't marry her!

GLAUCE

Why not?

JASON

I don't love her, for one.

GLAUCE

But you did—and you do,
And if you don't, you will.
You just don't know it yet.

JASON

I don't want to!

GLAUCE

Since when did that matter in love?

The truth is, you're two different bands
Playing the same kind of music.
All you have to do
Is turn down the volume a little.
You're both too loud for each other,
That's all . . .

JASON

I hate her guts!

GLAUCE

No you don't.
You admire them.
You have for 3,000 years
Because you've got the strength
To match hers.
She knows
She can't eat you,
And you can't eat her . . .

JASON
Laughing

You want a marriage of sharks . . .

AETES

Exactly.
Strength makes respect,
And where there's respect,
There's always a chance for love . . .

JASON
Startled

You want me to love her?

GLAUCE

Yes—'cause I think you do.

SHE SMILES.

Now go and be the brave man I know you are
And do what has to be done . . .

JASON

I don't have to do that!
I don't love her.

GLAUCE
Seriously

Jason, your words and your actions
Promised her things you can't walk away from.
She
Had *your* children . . .
She gave you her body and soul . . .

SHE SUDDENLY LAUGHS.

Besides,
What better revenge than this?
One woman willingly passes
Her lover off to a rival!
Talk about burning!

JASON
Incredulous

You'd use me—just to get her?

GLAUCE
Laughing

Of course not.
Burning her's just a fringe benefit
Of doing the right thing.

SINCERELY

Jason, I really believe it.
Deep down you belong to her,
And not me.
I'm not going to spend the rest of my life
Not being Medea.
I want to be me.

JASON
Exasperated

God, you're being a bitch!

GLAUCE

Exactly.
The truth is, inside every woman
There's a real bitch
Ready to wake up . . .

Leave her alone.
You're a man,
You don't—you can't—understand,
But she's there,
And you'll never figure her out
'Cause she doesn't think like you!

She's like Cerebus, my old wolf-hound,
Don't poke her—
'Cause hell's to pay when you do . . .

JASON
Challenging

You're like Medea?
I don't believe it!

GLAUCE

Medea and I are both women.
There's only one difference:
Her bitch is out of control
And mine's not.
Her bitch calls the shots
And drags *her* around on a chain!
Her, and her feminazis.

When she gets her bitch under control
She'll be right as rain.

JASON

So you won't marry me—ever?

GLAUCE

No.
Never.
I'm not going to spend my life
Locked in a cage called 'not being Medea',
'Cause it wouldn't be long
'Til my inner bitch breaks loose
And comes after you.

Trust me.
It's for the best.
This way you and I
Get sweet 'might have been's'.
The other way we'd get hell.

JASON
Hangs his head.

So it's finished with us?

GLAUCE

Yes.
But not between you and her.

JASON

She burned you alive!

GLAUCE

I know—but that's over now!

LAUGHS

I only burned for ten minutes.
She'll burn for ten thousand years!

MEDEA

Bitch!

GLAUCE

You ought to know . . .

IAN
Stepping into the fray

Well, how about it Jason.
You heard the word,
So let's move along
And make yours and Medea's
Deepest dreams come true!

JASON

Our nightmares you mean.

IAN

Nightmares are dreams too,
Just the negatives of your secret hopes and desires.

JASON

Whatever.
But I'm not doing this.

IAN

Why?

JASON

'Cause I want her to rot
In her feminist swamp.
I want her to stew
In that witches' brew
She unleashed on me and all men,
And choke on her own poison.
That's what I want.

IAN

And that will make you happy?

JASON

You bet!

IAN

Well marry her then,
That'll do it.

GLAUCE

If she rots,
You'll rot in it too, Jason.
You're part of her life.
Whatever happens to her
Happens to you!

JASON

What makes you think I can save her?

AETES

Because you're the kind of guy
Who does whatever it takes
To save *himself!*

MEDEA

Does anyone care about me in all this?
Or am I just something
Others play with—
Like women have always been?

GLAUCE

Well actually, we're all working hard on your happiness.

MEDEA

Don't.
I'll work on it by myself!

GLAUCE

Like you have all these years?

JASON

Don't worry Medea,
It 'ain't gonna' happen.
Not after what you did to our sons!

MEDEA

Shut up!
Shut
Up!

AETES
Defensively

She did that—
But after you booted her in the ass
Like she was some whore
And your sons were whore brats!

MEDEA

Shut up!
You can't talk about me like that,
I'm not just a thing!

JASON
Shouting

I left 'cause she made my life hell!
She went crazy with hatred for men!

MEDEA
Screaming loudly

Help me! Help!
Rape!
Ra-a-a-a-pe!

THE OTHERS FREEZE, SHOCKED, AND SURPRISED.

MEDEA
Scolding the audience

How dare you all sit there
While these slaves of phallocentric oppression
Rape me in public?
How dare you?
Listen!
Can't you hear how they use
Their misogynist tongues
As raping tools,
Thrusting their words
Like poisoned semantic ejaculate
Into my ears?
How can you just sit there
And let them do this to me?

It's outrageous
And I am outraged,
Absolutely outraged.
These men,

These fascist pimps who have lived off the labour of women,
These patriarchal rape-masters
And their co-opted, collaborationist bitch
Dare to discuss me
And my life
As if I were only a thing,
And without my permission!

GLAUCE

Sweetie, the whole damn world
Turns you without your permission.
Get over it.

MEDEA
Ignoring her; proclaiming to the audience

This is pornography!
The objectification of women
For the sadistic
Eroto-linguistic pleasure
Of men.

A woman is not just a colonized space,
We are not passive objects,
Fetish commodities
For capital-rapist material bondage,
Blank books, tabla rasas
Imprinted by men
With penis pens
And the semen ink
Spewed
From their logocentric testicles!

TURNING TO GLAUCE

Free yourself from your slavery
To them and their patriarchal
Testosterone-poisoned hegemony!

GLAUCE
Laughing

Talk about gas!
I'll bet you even fart editorials!

MEDEA
Self-righteously

Admit it.
Truth hurts.

GLAUCE
Laughing

It might—if I knew what it meant.

You know why you talk like that?
If you said it in simple English
You'd just die laughing before you finished a sentence.
I mean, 'phallocentric hegemony'—?
God!
You've got more pricks on the brain
Than a teenage slut!
You just dress it in fancier talk.

AS IF WHISPERING A SECRET, FORBIDDEN QUESTION IN CONFIDENCE.

Could it be *penis-envy?*

SHE LAUGHS; THEN, TO THE AUDIENCE.

I had penis-envy when I was little.
I could see right away
Peeing with a hose thingie
Was simpler than squatting.

Of course, I got over it after a while.
But some women never do,
And spend their whole lives
Bitching about it,
Always pissed off about men
For something or other.

SUDDENLY SERIOUS, TO JASON.

Jason, you said she was crazy with man-hate.
In that case, why did you leave her
Alone with two little boys?
You knew she's already killed
Her young brother . . .

JASON STANDS SILENTLY

AETES

She—and I'll never deny it—
She slit her own children's throats.
But you—goddamnit!—
You put the knife on the table.

Tell me, Jason,
Where was your world famous cunning then?
Where was your genius
For seeing and planning ahead?
How come your brilliance
Couldn't save your sons?

PAUSES.

But I've already told you why—
You're a pirate.
You can't be trusted to have a kingdom
Because you can't rule for all—
You can only steal for yourself.
I can't image a village of idiots
Wanting you for a king!

JASON

There's lots you can't imagine,
But it happens anyway.
That's what makes you so old.
And tired.

AETES

And you'll always be a green boy.

JASON

Green and flexible . . .

AETES

But without fruit
And that's what counts in this world,
The fruit
That you leave behind.
'Cause no one stays green forever.

JASON
Contemptuously

And what are you leaving behind?
A ruined kingdom,
A murdered son,
A runaway man-hating daughter—
You advertise your wares poorly, old man.

AETES

I leave behind me a vision
Of an old man
Not afraid to begin again
After losing everything,
An old man who swallows his pride
For the sake of the future . . .

MEDEA
Forcefully to the audience

There's something I want to get straight.
For the record.
About the death of my children.

I didn't *want* to do that.
I was crazy,
And scared.
—Yes! I was afraid—
I had nowhere to go in this world.
Sure, I had magic
But magic isn't a home,
It's not a place
Where somebody wants you.
And so I was desperate—
Heart-broken.

I didn't think he would leave me.
Then suddenly, I'm no longer his wife,
The mother of his two sons,
I was only his whore,
His fuck-bucket 'til something better arrived.
And she did . . .

JASON
Contemptuously

Bullshit!

MEDEA
Ignoring him; she moves closer to the audience to cut him off

I was so pissed off—
But not just with him.
With me!
For being so stupid!
I wanted to hurt *myself*
Just as much as him,
And what better way to do it
Than murder my children?

JASON

This is all bullshit.
She's trying to build an excuse
For killing her kids!

AETES

Understanding is not excusing.

MEDEA
Ignoring them

Have you ever been so mad at yourself
You felt like pounding your hand
Into mush with a hammer?
I would have done that to my heart,
That's how I felt.
Like quivering mush.
So I killed them,
'Cause there was no better way
To punish myself . . .

JASON
Sarcastic

Well, killing *them's* a hell of a way to do it!

MEDEA

I was crazy.
My inner bitch had broken her chain
It had nothing to do with them!

JASON
Sarcastic

Try telling them that.

MEDEA

I have—
For 3,000 years.

JASON
Presenting the children's words in a mocking tone.

And what do they say?
'We forgive you mommy
For slitting our throats
And drowning us in our blood?
We forgive you for using
Our bodies as pillows to stand on?'

MEDEA

No, you bastard,
They don't say that!

JASON

No?
So what do they say?

MEDEA
Bitterly

Nothing, you prick!
Not a thing in 3,000 years.

JASON

What did you expect—
Forgiveness?

MEDEA

No.

JASON

What then?

MEDEA

Nothing.
I just wanted them both to know
It was *my* fault,
Not theirs.

JASON

They knew that.

MEDEA

I wanted them
To hear it from me.

JASON
Sarcastic

There's a sweet comfort.

GLAUCE
In a warning tone.

Jason . . .

MEDEA

It was no fucking comfort at all.
There is no comfort
For those betrayed by their mothers.

JASON

So what's the point of all these . . . 'heroics'?
These . . . lurid confessions?

MEDEA

I wanted them both to know
Why it happened.
And that I was crazy
And didn't mean it,
And I'd do anything
To take it all back.

JASON

They must have been thrilled to hear that.
I'll bet they can hardly wait
To see you again.

GLAUCE
Pleading

Jason, would you shut up?
Just this one time,
Please . . .

JASON

What's the matter—
She grab your heart-strings?

GLAUCE

Yes.

JASON

So you feel sorry for her?

GLAUCE

There's not a woman alive
Who'd want to be her shoes,
And doesn't feel sorry for her.

JASON

Why?
She murdered her children on purpose.

GLAUCE

Yes, but she didn't mean to—
Not kill them forever.

JASON

Killing is always 'forever',
And deep down inside,
She isn't sorry a bit.
Haven't you seen her
Encourage millions of women
To murder their children too—
While they're still in the womb?

If she was really sorry
She wouldn't do that . . .

She doesn't say,
'I speak as a woman
Who's murdered two of her children.
See how it's twisted my soul?
Like an old rag,
And turned my blood into dirty dish-water.'

No,
Instead she encourages others
To commit the same crime,
'Cause misery loves company.

GLAUCE

You've lost your faith in nature,
Haven't you, Jason?
Do you think any woman
—Even Medea—
Could spend 3,000 years
Remembering how she murdered her children
And stay the same?
Do you think those women who kill their unborn
Don't feel the horror now and again?

JASON

You're such a fine woman
You can't imagine
Things like Medea exist.
Look, Glauce, I've killed men,
Lots of them,
But every last man I killed
Could have killed me.
I've never shredded a baby
And anybody who does
Deserves being peeled alive
With a fruit-knife . . .

STOPS, BREATHING HARD, THEN CHALLENGINGLY.

Look at her. She's a monster.

GLAUCE

Not when she loved you enough
To betray her country,
And murder her brother for you.

JASON

You make it sound like a virtue.

GLAUCE

I'm a woman Jason.
Whatever is done for love
Has some virtue mixed in.
To us love and virtue are one and the same.

JASON

She murdered her sons.
She burned you alive!

GLAUCE

For love.

JASON

You're joking.
For love?

GLAUCE

For frustrated, wounded,
Totally heart-broken love—
Which is still
Love . . .

JASON

That doesn't make it right.

GLAUCE

No, but it makes it understandable.

JASON

I don't want to understand.

GLAUCE

There's your problem.

JASON

My problem?

GLAUCE

Partly.
And mine.
We helped put her in down in the hell
Where child-killer mothers go.

JASON

We?
Now I suppose we helped kill the kids . . .

GLAUCE

Jason, don't be a jerk.
We didn't kill the kids.

She took the knife—
And everything else.
But Aetes is right.
We put the knife on the table . . .

JASON
Somewhat shocked

You really believe that?

GLAUCE

I do.

JASON

So Ovid was right?
We shouldn't have fallen in love?

GLAUCE

Don't be ridiculous!
Falling in love was no crime
But wanting to marry was.
You already had a wife.

JASON

You didn't think so then.

GLAUCE

I've had 3,000 years
Of watching you both
To think it over.

You haven't stopped thinking of her
In 3,000 years!

JASON
Shocked

Are you saying I love her?

GLAUCE

Yes.

JASON

More than I love you.

GLAUCE

Yes.

JASON

We've been fighting for 3,000 years!

GLAUCE

Not a fight, Jason,
A lover's quarrel,
The craziest kind of quarrel there is.
Part real, and part game,
All aimed at kiss and make up.

Deep down inside you never
Wanted to leave her for good.

Things went that way
Because *I just happened* to be there
To bandage your wounds.

I was too young to know
The difference between
A real fight and quarreling lovers . . .

*SHE LOOKS DOWN, OBVIOUSLY DEJECTED BY HER
CONFESSION.*

JASON

Maybe that's how it started
But that's not how it is now.

GLAUCE

Now more than ever.

JASON
After a pause; mystified and somewhat hurt.

Why are you suddenly saying all this?

GLAUCE

Because I am not
The Golden Fleece.

JASON
Deeply puzzled

What the hell does that mean?

GLAUCE

> After Iolcus,
> More than anything else,
> You wanted to be a king.
> And then you saw me,
> But Corinth was half my beauty, Jason,
> And I was only the other half of the prize.

JASON
Angry and desperate

> You're crazy!
> Totally, fucking crazy!
> I love you because you're natural.
> You accept yourself as a woman
> And me as a man.
> Not like Medea and all her Bitches
> Rejecting nature,
> Like Amazons cutting off tits
> To make themselves something they're not.
>
> But not you.
> And that's why I love you.
> And that's why you're happy,
> Like me:
> Because I accept myself
> As Nature made me—

MEDEA

> A rapist!

GLAUCE
Exasperated

Oh for God's sake!
Both of you—
Get off the soap-box,
And deal with the subject—
You!

AETES

Exactly.
So, what's your choice, boy,
A pirate, or king?

GLAUCE

With me you'll be a pirate forever,
With her, you might turn into a king.

JASON

What makes you say that?

GLAUCE

I've already said it,
To you I'm not real.
I'm just 'not Medea',
A kind of bright shadow,
But still a shadow, my dear.
And she'll always be standing behind me,
A haunting, bitter, dark eminence
Secretly ruling my life . . .

I need

—And *you* need—
Real love to be who you are,
Not the dancing shadows we'd be.
Your pirating days are over, Jason.
You're going to marry Medea,
To be a king,
And I'm the best bridesmaid ever—
I'm giving away the bride.

SHE SMILES AT HIM.

JASON HANGS HIS HEAD, EYES CLOSED, BREATHING DEEPLY A FEW TIMES. HE SEEMS LOST IN THOUGHT, OR IN DESPERATE SCHEMING.

JASON

I'll never stop fighting her!
Wherever she goes with her poison,
I'll be there!

GLAUCE

Jason, life is *not* war.

JASON
Vehemently

Life *is* war!
Nature is war
The fittest survive,
And we're part of nature,
So therefore, our lives are war:
Takers and taken,
Winners and whiners,
Eaters and eaten,

That's it, Glauce,
Life's bottom line.

GLAUCE

Perhaps,
But our job is to rise above nature,
Like trees rise out of the ground,
Up, to the sun.
We're not lions
Killing their young,
Or eagles, letting their weakest ones starve . . .

JASON

To keep the breed strong, Glauce,
To keep it fit . . .

AETES

Well, that leaves you out, now doesn't it?
Your children are dead.
One more time you're a loser.

JASON
Pointing to Glauce

She and I could have changed that.

AETES

Could have—but didn't.
'Could have' doesn't get medals
And doesn't pass on his genes . . .
Face it—loser!

JASON

You're talking?
What have you got?
A dead son,
A broken down kingdom,
A psycho-path daughter
And no Golden Fleece.

AETES
Gesturing to the audience

Look around you, Jason.
Not one of those people out there
Believe in the Golden Fleece,
The nice ones think it's a fabulous story,
The softies think it's a symbol of mystical truth,
And the cynics think it's a clever phrase
For Medea's crotch.

JASON
Snarling

Who gives a damn what they think?

AETES

That's pirate talk, boy,
Free-loaders,
And hit and run lovers,
But aren't you the one
Who wants to be king?
Who wants a country to rule?

188

Now, you've l~~
So if you ~~
These [*The gestures to the theatre audience*] are your people now.
You've got to make it with them.
Because these are the only people you'll ever have.
They are your future.
Set them a good example,
Lead them well—
'Cause if you lose them
You'll less than a ghost—
Just a bunch of words on a page.

They want you married, Jason.
That's why they came here today.
They came here to see
The war between you two ended.
They've had enough of the gender wars.
They don't give a damn why they started,
They just want them over.

GLAUCE

By God do we ever!

HECABE
Calmly, with great dignity.

Yes, indeed.
By God, do we ever.

PAUSES AND THEN ADDRESSES THE AUDIENCE.

None of you know who I am.
If the histories name me at all
I am called, 'the Queen',
King Aetes' queen

But my name is Hecabe,
And like my daughter Medea,
I am a moon-priestess,
And know the ceremonies of women
And the rites of our mother, the sea.

I have watched, and said nothing
For 3,000 years.
But now through this actress,
I will have my say,
And I know that I speak for many.

If Jason is still like a little boy
Running around, playing pirates,
Medea is still a small girl
Stuck in the playground wars.

Remember them?
Girls versus boys?
Boys versus girls?
When we really believed
In boy-germs and girl-germs
And if you touched one of *them*, you were dirty
And had to wash quick
Or get sick
And maybe you'd even die!

SHE SMILES.

I remember
We had this 'magical' verse
To purify any girl who'd been touched by a boy,
"Sugar and spice,
And pretty girls' song,
Boy dirt, boy dirt
Gone, gone, gone!"

We really believed it!

SHE SMILES.

That's what the gender wars are,
The playground wars gone way over-time,
With little girls like Medea
Still hiding inside their girl forts,
Still chanting
"Sugar and spice,
And pretty girls' song,
Boy dirt, boy dirt
Gone, gone, gone!"

Of course, they don't say it like that anymore.
They write fat books
With fine-sounding titles,
You know, like
"Introduction to Post-semantic, Sub-Patriachal Pre-
   dialectical Gender Theory"
And "Equality as a Synergy of Patriarchal Oppression",
But it all comes down to one thing,
"Boy dirt, boy dirt, gone, gone, gone!"

IN A PARODY OF MR. ROGERS.

Can we do better than that boys and girls?

I knew we could.

SHE STOPS AND TAKES ON A MORE SERIOUS TONE.

Women don't want their men
Turned into the enemy,
Sons, and husbands, fathers and brothers,

Our sons-in-law and our grand-sons
Demonized,
Medicalized,
As if maleness were a disease
And needed a 'cure'
To fix Mother Nature's blunder.

Only fools believe
They know better than Nature,
And Jason is right:
Such pride
Invites a hard fall.

Besides, how could we love such scum
Without being scum ourselves?
Loving such a disease
Makes us part of the sickness.

MEDEA

Ex-actly!

HECABE
Ignoring her, to the audience

If all our foremothers were only
Whipped women and weak, blind fools
Who never learned how to handle a man,
What does that make us, their daughters?

If all our forefathers
Were cruel, woman-hating monsters,
What makes us think that we,
Their daughters, can be much better?

You can't make silk purses
Out of sows' ears.
It's really quite simple:
Garbage in, garbage out!

And if we're all trash
Does it matter who's running the show?
Why all this fussing
To put new garbage on top?

No dump gets better
Just by replacing
One bag of trash
With another.

MEDEA
Hissing

Traitor!

HECABE
Passionately turns on Medea

No, not a traitor—a woman!
Who wants what women
Have always wanted—
Everything!
Everything we can get—
So long as it doesn't endanger
Our bottom line:
Family.

We'll grab whatever we can
As long as we can hang on
To children,
And husbands.

When it gets down to that
We start making trades-offs . . .

MEDEA
Sneering

You mean, you start to surrender.
Well, not any more,
We've come a long way, baby!

HECABE

Maybe not you, but others have heard
Their unborn children are calling,
And those children need fathers,
Real fathers—
Not just a shot of sperm.

They want Jason to stop playing pirate
And start playing house.

MEDEA
Scoffing

Slaves running back to their chains!

HECABE

They're going where happiness takes them!

MEDEA

Piss on happiness!

HECABE

Every kill-joy and every fanatic
Says the same thing.
That's why they spread
So much misery:
They want to make the whole world
As unhappy as they are.

MEDEA
Aggressively

Freedom
And pride come first.

GLAUCE

What pride is there in unhappiness?

HECABE

Freedom for what, Medea?
What are you for?

MEDEA

Women!

HECABE

Women as they are—
Or women
As *you* want them to be?

MEDEA

Women as they *can* be,
Free women!

HECABE

Your kind of freedom
Is nothing but terrible two's—
Tantrums, and biting
And always wanting your way.

GLAUCE

Good horsemanship
Is a matter of trade-offs
Between rider and horse.
Only the gods get it all.

MEDEA
Contemptuously; dismissively

That's what all losers say, *horse-girl.*

GLAUCE
Angry; she counts out on her fingers as she speaks

Loser? Me?
Ha!
You've lost your parents,
Your country,
Your brother,
Your husband
Your good name

And your sons—
And you talk to about 'losers'?

RUMMAGING THROUGH HER PURSE.

Here—let me get you a mirror!

MEDEA
Snarling

I didn't lose them.
I *threw* them away.

HECABE

More the fool you.

MEDEA

They were links in my chain.

GLAUCE

They were links to your life.

MEDEA

They kept me down.

GLAUCE

They kept you connected
And human.

HECABE
Trying to divert this growing cat-fight

THE GENDER WARS TRILOGY

Medea, you want to make changes,
But surely you know
Sewing with nails instead of needles,
Makes a worse mess
Than doing nothing at all.

MEDEA
Disdainfully

Mother, you know damn well
I never bothered with sewing.

HECABE
Slightly annoyed

You never bothered with anything
But *yourself.*
That's why you think
We're all just like you.

MEDEA
Self-righteously

I've set a good example.

GLAUCE

Of acting like men at their worst.

HECABE

Most women find
Persuasion is how we work best.

MEDEA

That's how they turn themselves into whores!

HECABE
Gently

Medea, my dear,
It's time you grew up and learned
There's a bit of a whore
In every woman.
There's a bit of a john
In every man . . .

MEDEA

A bit of a rapist, you mean.

HECABE

A bit, but whores know how to work that
To their advantage.

MEDEA
Outraged

You'd admit it?
Here?
In front of your husband?

HECABE

It doesn't matter if I admit it or not.
He knows,
And every man knows.

And what's more,
They like it.

MEDEA

Outrageous!

GLAUCE

Yes, but it's worked very well
For millions of years,
And kept us alive,
Even though humans
Are naked and weak.

HECABE

It gave our foremothers
Plenty of leverage
Just as Nature intended.

MEDEA

Men can take that!
They always have!
And they always will!

HECABE
Appalled

My God, you're really a child,
Still on the playground!

Women are not as helpless as you've been preaching,
Nor men as heartless.

The truth is,
Men *want* to pay,
They *like* pleasing women,
They *like* being wanted.

GLAUCE

Why do you think every hooker
Puts on a good show?

MIMICKING.

"Oh honey, oh ba-a-a-aby!
I need you so bad . . ."

And every rapist
Convinces himself she wants it.

MEDEA

I don't want some man wanting me!

HECABE
Seriously

Only the mad
Don't want to be wanted.
Only the mad
Think they need only themselves.

MEDEA

Wanting us—
That's how they lock us in cages—
Called 'marriage.'

HECABE

Marriage, my dear,
Is Mother Nature's invention
To raise the odds of survival
For poor little naked apes
With no teeth and no claws.
It's as simple as that.

GLAUCE
Mock despair and/or annoyance

Oh for God's sake—
You haven't figured it out?

*SHE GOES RIGHT UP TO MEDEA AND, STILL USING
HER FINGERS TO EMPHASIZE 'SHE', 'HIM' ETC,
EXPLAINS IT TO HER.*

Look, it's *so* easy:
She promises *him*
All the kids are his.
And *he* promises *her*
To provide and protect,
Especially against human predators

That way she can focus
On poor little naked apes
That need constant care.
And that way he knows *for sure*
They're *his*
So he'll hang around
And do whatever it takes
To keep her and the kids alive.

LIKE A LECTURER REACHING A CONCLUSION.

> She gives him sex for love,
> And he gives her love for sex.
> It's beautiful in its simplicity,
> And in 4 million years
> We haven't found anything better.

MEDEA

> I can! And I will!

HECABE

> Your pride has driven you mad.

MEDEA

> Me? Crazy?
> How dare you?
> I'm a free woman
> And you—a self-confessed slave!

HECABE
Self-defensive at first and then increasingly aggressive

> I may be enslaved
> But at least it's to a *real* man,
> And for all my sorrows
> I've lived a *real* life—
> But you—*you* are enslaved
> To little-girl playground fantasies—
>
> Your lunatic 'herstory'
> As it never was,
> Filled with women and men

As they never were,
And a future
That never can be
With people as they are not—
You live in cloud-cuckoo-land
And babble in cloud-cuckoo language,
And all it boils down to is
"Boy dirt, boy dirt, gone, gone, gone!"

Like Jason,
You just don't want to grow up!

MEDEA
With a hint of desperation

You're fucking crazy!

HECABE
Severely

Say that again
And I'll slap your tongue
Back into your mouth
And paste your face on the moon.
I may only be your mother,
But I
Am also your Queen,
And you are my subject.

MEDEA SAYS NOTHING. HECABE CONTINUES MORE QUIETLY.

I know your name, Rumpelstilskin—
'*Woman-hater*'!

The greatest woman hater of all!

Because you can't accept yourself
As nature made us.
You want to force us into the cage *you've* made,
So you can whip us
Into *your* party-line,
And re-shape us
In *your* image,
To *your* preferences—
The preferences of a little girl, still singing,
"Boy dirt, boy dirt, gone, gone, gone!"

*MEDEA LAUGHS, BUT IT IS A HOLLOW, FORCED
LAUGHTER THAT CLEARLY TELLS THE AUDIENCE
THAT HECABE HAS STRUCK HOME. SHE THEN
SHOUTS,*

MEDEA

I want women to be free!
Free to be and do *whatever* they want!

GLAUCE

That kind of freedom doesn't exist!
When the spoon tries to be a knife
It makes a fool of itself.

HECABE
Dismissively

You only want women free to be *you*!
That's not the same thing as wanting them free.

You don't want us out of cages,
You want us into *your* cage!

Well, your dreams are the sheerest piffle!
In a power struggle with men,
We lose.
Do you know why?
Because we only win
As long as the men play by *our* rules.
When push comes to shove,
Even your new age guys
Can push and shove harder
Than any of us.

So what do you do?
Instead of facing the fact
Persuasion is all we've got,
You concoct these lunatic 'herstories' to explain
Why we're not
Like you think we should be.

Why should we follow a woman
Who has no love for herself
As a woman?

MEDEA

Because I will lead you to glory!

GLAUCE

By stomping all over our men?
No thanks.

HECABE
Pulling herself together

Medea, I speak to you now as a woman.
You owe me two children.

You murdered my son Absyrtus,
And nothing can bring him back
Or heal the wound in my heart.
But a child from you
—Be it a grandson or daughter—
Will bring me new joys
To help me live with my grief.

And you owe me a child
For the one I lost when you murdered
Your brother Absyrtus.
Nothing can bring her back
But a child from you
—Be it a grandson or daughter—
Will bring me new joys
To help me live with my grief.

I declare before all that is holy to women,
Love, the heart, motherhood,
And the wisdom and power
Of our all-mother, the sea,
You owe me a debt of life,
And if you do not pay it,
I will do nothing but stand forever
Before all the world
And proclaim through the ages
Your child-debt to me.

You may scold me and shout me down,
But I will continue to speak
And add my voice to your shoutings
Until one day
Even you hear it:
You owe me two children.

SHE TURNS TO JASON.

Jason, I speak as a mother.
You owe me two children.
For you she murdered my son,
And doing so killed herself.
I want my son and daughter back, Jason,
I know you can't do that.
What's done is done,
But you can give me new joys
To let me live with the grief.

You claim you don't love her,
But with Glauce I say
You don't know your own heart.
A quarrel of 3,000 years
Can only be fueled by love,
A childish, immature love
But a love that can grow—and grow up.

JASON
Almost defiantly

And you think I'm just going to do that?

HECABE

Yes.

JASON

Why should I?

HECABE

Because you really don't have a choice.
And neither does she.

JASON

No choice?
Watch me.

HE TURNS AWAY AND STARTS TO WALK OUT. AFTER HESITATING A FEW MOMENTS, MEDEA, THOUGH KEEPING SOME DISTANCE FROM JASON, WALKS OUT AS WELL. THEY ARE JUST AT THE DOOR OF THE THEATRE WHEN TWO YOUNG MEN STAND UP.

CADMUS

Father!

PENTHEUS

Mother!

JASON AND MEDEA STAND FROZEN. THEY DO NOT EVEN TURN AROUND.

CADMUS

Wait!

PENTHEUS

Don't go!

CADMUS

Don't you remember us?

PENTHEUS

Don't you want to see us?

THEY MOVE TOWARDS THEIR PARENTS. MEDEA TURNS AROUND, SEES THEM AND, WITH AN UTTERLY HORRIFIED LOOK ON HER FACE, STAGGERS, CLUTCHING AT THE AIR FOR SUPPORT, UNTIL FINALLY SHE TOUCHES JASON, WHO TAKES HER AND HOLDS HER UP. THE BOYS STAND IN FRONT OF THEM, ALSO APPREHENSIVE, WAITING TO SEE WHAT HAPPENS. MEDEA STILL HANGS ON TO JASON, SHIELDING HER FACE FROM HER SONS, BOTH OF WHOM HAVE A RED STREAK ACROSS THEIR THROATS. THE OTHER CHARACTERS, AETES, GLAUCE, HECABE, IAN ARE GATHERED AROUND.

JASON

I would hug you, boys,
But as you can see
Your mother's not well right now.

CADMUS

I understand.

PENTHEUS
Reaches out and touches Medea

Mother?
Are you all right?

MEDEA
Looking up

Pentheus?

PENTHEUS

Yes, mother. It's me.

MEDEA HIDES HER FACE AGAIN.

CADMUS

It's Cadmus, mother.
Look at me, please . . .

HE REACHES OUT AND TOUCHES HER. AFTER A FEW MOMENTS, SHE HESITANTLY LOOKS UP AND THEN, VERY SLOWLY, CAREFULLY REACHES OUT TO TOUCH HIS HAND. FOR A FEW MOMENTS SHE HOLDS HIS HAND, THEN TAKES THE HAND THAT PENTHEUS HAS OFFERED. AFTER A FEW MOMENTS MEDEA SEPARATES FROM JASON AND STANDS HOLDING THE HANDS OF THE TWO BOYS WHOM SHE MURDERED.

MEDEA
Looking down

I'm sorry.

CADMUS

We know.

MEDEA

I feel ashamed.

PENTHEUS

We know.

MEDEA

I was insane.
Angry.
Humiliated.
Hurt.
Frightened.

CADMUS

We know—
But you are still our mother,
Even the most terrible moment
Cannot undo that.

PENTHEUS

One horrible moment of weakness—
Among many good.
We cannot forget what happened,
But we can choose what we want to dwell on.

MEDEA

How can you forgive me?

PENTHEUS

We cannot.
You'll have to forgive yourself—
If you can.
All we can do is say we are ready
To go on to something better.

MEDEA

It sounds foolish,
But if I can do anything . . .

*BOTH BOYS STAND SILENTLY LOOKING AT MEDEA
AS THE OTHER CHARACTERS DRAW IN CLOSER.
MEDEA LOOKS AT HER SONS, THEN AT JASON.
THERE ARE LONG MOMENTS OF INTENSE SILENCE
AS THE AUDIENCE CAN ALMOST HEAR JASON AND
MEDEA STRUGGLING WITHIN THEMSELVES TO THE
CONCLUSION.*

MEDEA
Breathing deeply, drawing herself up, with dignity.

Jason, if you will marry me,
I will marry you.

JASON
After a few moments

I will marry you
If you will marry me.

IAN
Quickly

I now pronounce you man and wife!

You may kiss!

*THEY DO NOT KISS, BUT GRASP EACH OTHER'S ARM
MORE TIGHTLY. THEN THEY STAND WITH THEIR
CHILDREN BETWEEN THEM. IAN RAISES THE
REPLICA OF THE DOUBLE-AXE OVER THEM.*

This marriage has taken place
Under the sign of the great double-axe,
To which I now draw your attention.

There is only one axe,
But there are two blades
Facing in different directions,
One being,
Two ways,
But always together
Inseparable,
Equal,
Distinct.
Joined,
But different.

If you try to split it
You will get only dangerous halves.

One axe,
Two blades,
Symbols of mutual respect

And power
Ready to take on the world.

An axe is serious business,
Not a toy,
Not for games,
So choose well
How you use it,
To build
Or destroy.

Treat it with care.
Keep it clean.
Even steel
Needs the oil of love
To stay sharp
And rustless.

Reflect on this symbol
Which reminds you: this world
Is one process,
With two aspects,
Yin and yang,
Female and male,
Spirit and matter,
Yes and no,
Light and dark,
And the two are tied in a knot
So subtle
That none can undo it.
What God has joined
No one can pull asunder.
Those who try
Will only destroy themselves.

Eden is always behind us.
We in this age, above all
Are pioneering into a new country
Carrying with us the symbol
Of new sober purpose,
The great double-axe
To build ourselves
Another new home
In the journey that lasts forever.

*EXIT ALL IN A PROCESSION TO THE SOUND OF
WAGNER'S "RIDE OF THE VALKYRIES."*

BVG